OLD CEYLON

OLD CEYLON

SKETCHES OF CEYLON LIFE IN THE OLDEN TIME

JOHN CAPPER

GYAN

Published by

Gyan Publishing House
5, Ansari Road
Daryaganj, New Delhi-110002
Phone: 011-47034999, 9811692060
E-mail: books@gyanbooks.com

Distribution Network
gyanbooks.com
India, USA, Canada, UK, Australia

ISBN: 978-93-7169-164-2 (PB)

First Published, 1878

2nd Impression 2025

Printed at: Gyan Press, Delhi.

OLD CEYLON

Author: JOHN CAPPER

THE VALE OF DUMBERA.

OLD CEYLON.

SKETCHES OF CEYLON LIFE IN THE OLDEN TIME:

BY

JOHN CAPPER,

AUTHOR OF THE "THREE PRESIDENCIES OF INDIA,"
THE "GOLD FIELDS," &c., &c.

WITH ILLUSTRATIONS BY CEYLON ARTISTS.

LONDON: MESSRS. W. B. WHITTINGHAM & CO.
ABERDEEN: MESSRS. A. & R. MILNE.

1878.

MANY of the following Sketches were published in the early volumes of DICKENS' "HOUSEHOLD WORDS," more than a quarter of a century ago. Some are now given for the first time, but nearly all refer to a period between thirty and forty years ago.

In the hope that these Pictures of "OLD CEYLON" may be acceptable to some of those who take an interest in our beautiful island, they are now brought together, so that the memory of bye-gone times may not pass away for ever.

COLOMBO, *September*, 1877.

CONTENTS.

ILLUSTRATIONS.

THE GARDEN OF FLOWERS.

THE Coffee Estate on which I resided was situated in one of the wildest and most beautiful districts of the island of Ceylon, elevated far above the luxuriant lowlands, where fragrant spices and waving palms told of wide plains and balmy winds. The plantation was on a broad table-land, fully three thousand five hundred feet above the sea level, many miles removed from the only European town in the interior, and at least five miles from any other white man's dwelling. Within a short walk of the lower boundary of my property, was a small Kandyan village containing within itself the very pith and essence of Cingalese society, a true type of the native community of the interior. As I mixed so unreservedly and frequently with the people, and saw so much of their every-day-life, it may be interesting to give a faint outline of this little hamlet.

Malwattie, which was its name, signifies literally, a "garden of flowers," and such in truth it was, when I first visited it. Unlike any European village, there was not such a thing as a row of houses or huts to be seen: shops were unknown in that primitive place, and until later years, no such incubus as a tavern keeper or renter was known there. Every little hut or cottage was carefully shaded from the view of its neighbour, fairly established on its own account, as much so, as though the inmates had written up in barbarous Cingalese characters, "No connexion with the house next door." I never could learn that there was any superstition among native hut builders, as to the variation in the aspect of their domiciles, but certain it was that no two dwellings faced precisely the same points of the compass. One would be north-east, and the nearest to it would be north-east and by east: you might fancy you had found another facing a similar point, but on careful observation you would see that you could not make it any better than north-east-and-by-east-half-east. I tried the experiment for a long time, but was compelled at length, to give it up, I had regularly "boxed the compass" round the entire village, but in vain.

Partly from long established custom, and partly from a desire of shading their dwellings from the heat of the sun, the Kandyans bury their isolated huts beneath a dense mass of the rankest vegetation. At a short distance not a sign of human habitation could be traced, were it not for the thickly growing tops of bananas, areka palms, and bread-fruit trees, which are ever found around and above their quiet abodes.

Malwattie formed no exception to the general rule in this respect; it was as snugly hedged, and fenced, and grown over, as was Robinson Crusoe's dwelling after the visit of the savages. Every tiny hut appeared to possess a maze of its own for the express purpose of perplexing all new-comers, especially white men. The entire village did not cover more than an eighth of a square mile, yet it would have puzzled any living thing but a bird to have visited all the cottages in less time than half a day, and very giddy, trying work it would have been.

Small as was this primitive community, it had its superiors. The leading men were the priest ef the little Buddhist Vihara, or shrine; and the Korale or headman. I will not distress the reader by putting the names of these men in print, as they would be perfectly unpronounceable, and moreover, as lengthy as the approaches to their own dwellings. The entire names of one Cingalese community would fill a small sized volume. I will therefore, only speak of these persons as the Priest and the Korale.

The latter was a rather respectable man, as things go in Ceylon; he was negatively irreproachable in character. He had certainly never committed murder or theft on the Queen's highway. Perjury had not been charged against him, and as for the faithful discharge of his few official duties, no one had ever called that in question, though there were some rather curious tales afloat on the subject of the last assessment on rice lands. At the office of the Government Agent of the district he was believed to be as active and honest as nine-tenths of the native headmen, though to be sure that was not saying very much for him. The villagers looked up to him with the utmost veneration and respect, and no wonder, for on his fiat depended the amount of rice tax their lands were to pay. He was a venerable looking old gentleman, with a flowing white beard, a keen, quiet eye, and an easy-going habit that might have been called dignity or lazyness. It was his duty to render to the Government officers a just account of the industry, if such a term can be applied to any Cingalese, of his village; to furnish returns of the increase or decrease of the population; to give notice of all crimes and offences committed; and in short to represent the local government in minor details. For all this, no salary was paid him. He was satisfied with the honor of the office; and yet, strange to tell, this Korale had so far increased his property by gaining nothing, that he was a man of some substance when I left the place, owning some hundreds of cattle and rich in pasture lands. Education was unknown to him; he could scratch a little Cingalese on the dried leaves used in place of paper, and I believe could count as far as ten. His most complicated accounts were all on a decimal system, and by the aid of numerous symbols known but to himself and the erudition of the friendly priest, he contrived to transact a multitude of business with the authorities.

The abode of this old patriarch would have furnished a study for a lover of the antique. Everything seemed in keeping with his long white beard. The doors and windows, the couches and three-legged table, all were hoary with years. Even the atmosphere had a musty smell about it, as though it had been keeping him company ever since he was a little boy.

In the midst of thick foliage, as bright and green as the cottage was dark and cankery, it seemed at a distance, like a huge wart on the rich vegetation. The coffee, the bananas, the cotton, the jambo, the pau-pau grew in wild profusion. Of what we should call garden, he had none, nor did he need any, for the friendly villagers kept his daily wants amply supplied from their own poor scanty patches. At early dawn the little narrow pathway leading circuitously to his door, might be seen tracked by men, women and children, laden with fruit, vegetables, and eggs for the Korale's larder ; he might well grow stout and glossy and contented with his lot. There was such a supply of vegetable diet introduced through his crazy old doorway each morning, as might have fully satisfied the vegetarians of Great Britain, with something to spare for the pigs. But the old gentleman disposed of it all ; for he had a little colony of feudal dependants hanging about his heels behind his own barn of a place. These serfs tracked him wherever he went ; one held a paper umbrella or a talipot leaf over him in his walks : another carried his stick of office : one beat off the musquitoes ; another fanned him to sleep with a punkah. In short they did everything for him, save eat and sleep, and these functions he performed for himself to perfection.

The old Korale was generally pleased with my visits, for they added to his importance in the eyes of the little community. He lived quite alone ; his wife had been dead some years, and he had lost his only child by fever. His days were mostly passed in sleeping, smoking and eating, varied occasionally with a stroll round his rice fields, or those of his neighbours. It was seldom that he visited Kandy, the ancient capital : as for Colombo, the wildest freaks of imagination would never induce him to contemplate a journey so far from his domestic hearth.

It was a curious sight to behold this ancient being leading such a hedge-hog existence : rolling himself up in indolence, after every meal of rice and curry, in his little darkened, cavern-like verandah; and there, if no guest arrived, falling asleep until the next meal aroused him from his torpor, I have found him thus, clad in semi-barbaric pomp, reeking with dirt, and swelled with importance in a baloon-shaped Kandyan hat, a flowing robe and loose jacket with shoulder-of-mutton sleeves, secured by silver bangles; an enormous mass of white muslin wrapped, fold upon fold, around his waist. A petty little mountain stream fell trickling and bubbling past the door, over stones and sticks, and flowers and herbs, until it was lost in the rice fields below, playing and gambolling as though each tiny wave had been some frolicsome wood nymph. Little could be seen from that shady portal, and not much more heard, beyond the hum of myriad insects and the distant cry of jungle birds.

Often have I sat with the Korale chatting on local and other matters, for he was a man of gossip though of limited ideas. I tried in vain to make him understand the position and importance of other conntries: of their great superiority to the Kandyans, and of the features which distinguished us people of the west from orientals. He could not be persuaded that Europe was larger or a better place than Ceylon; that better corn and vegetables were grown in England, than on the Kandyan hills; or that a modern drawing-room was a more comfortable sort of place than a Cingalese Korale's reception room, with earthen floor and leafy ceiling. Of some description of politics he had gleaned a faint idea from the reported contents of one of the local newspapers very democratic in its principles. He had an inkling that things were not going on as they should do, and that a republic must be the sort of government suited to the present wants of man, yet strange to say he connected with his ideas of reform, a return to those things which the liberality of the British Government had abolished, forced labour and flogging at the discretion of the headmen!

The priest was of a far different stamp, not an educated man in any European sense of the word; but still with some glimmering of mind within, just serving to render internal darkness visible. He of course, could read fluently; for it was a portion of his duties to recite verses of their Pitakas or sacred writings, morning and evening in the Vihara. He possessed a fair share of curiosity, and a desire to know something of other places and things. Nay, more, he frequently heard me read a whole chapter of the Scriptures, with which he was much pleased and frankly admitted that Christianity was the best religion next to Buddhism.

His Vihara and dwelling were at one end of the range of little hills, on the slopes of which the village of Malwattie was situated, though above them considerably. It was the only roof covered by tiles; and, unlike the rest, might be seen at some distance peeping out from amidst a dense mass of foliage. To arrive at it the traveller had to wind his way along a weary length of loose stones that led over low swampy ground, round the edges of rice fields and up the sides of rather steep hills—a slip from which bid fair to plunge the wayfarer down some very ugly places. It was a path that should be trodden by none but a tight-rope dancer, or a native of the country.

The view from the door of the shrine was highly picturesque, commanding a survey of many miles of mountain, forest and prairie country, through which herds of cattle were dotted like so many very small mice. His abode was mean in the extreme, with scarce sufficient to make life supportable. The rules of his order forbad him to acquire any property, and he subsisted from day to day on charity—just as did his friend the Korale.

The priest often visited me on the plantation, and examined with much curiosity the various books and pictures about the bungalow. On one of these occasions an incident occurred which threatened at first to cut short our intimacy; but was eventually forgotten or laughed at. I had frequently pressed my yellow-robed friend to partake of my meal, and taste a little port wine, of which I knew most of these people are very fond—but in vain; he professed the utmost dislike to any strong drinks, independently of the restriction laid on them by their rules. One day while conversing with him, I was called away to the coffee store by one of the labourers, and left him alone, sitting by my little jungle sideboard. As I was returning immediately afterwards, and when near the door, I heard a great coughing and spluttering, and strange choking noises. Upon entering I found the priest almost dead with a fit of coughing. He staggered against the wall, his eyes were streaming with water, his hands clenched together, while down his long golden robes, a jet black stream had made its sable way. A bottle lay at his feet. The truth flashed across me in a moment. The wary priest had gone to my sideboard to steal a taste of the forbidden wine, and had, unfortunately, taken a good draught from a quart bottle of ink!

Next in importance to the characters already named, was one Ranghamy the head constable, deputy sheriff, tax collector and there is no saying what besides. He was the right hand man of the Korale, not quite so stout, but more thick headed, save when his own interest was concerned, and then it was remarkable how his faculties brightened up and illuminated the social atmosphere of Malwattie. Ranghamy was not a native of the village, nor of the district; none had ever known whence he came except the Korale, and he had long since forgotton. The hydra-headed official had a numerous progeny of Ranghamies of both sexes, besides a large herd of sleek, well-favoured cattle; yet, oddly enough, he had neither lands whereon to pasture the one, nor salary wherewith to feed and clothe the other, Still they were all fed, clothed and pastured. The junior head constable and the little female deputy sheriffs, and the tax collectors in arms were clad in whiter robes than any other young villagers. As for the cattle they might have been exhibited at the Smithfield show, and won all the prizes by several stone of fat. Whether they grew thus corpulent from any miraculous interference of Buddha, or were fattened by some scientific process upon a few constables' broken staves and collector's decayed tax books, or whether they were daily driven upon other peoples' lands who dared not complain to the Korale, and if they did, could not expect the head constable to impound his own bullocks, which of these might have been the case, I never learnt, though I had my suspicions in the matter. Ranghamy was said to have realised considerable sums by hiring out his cattle to the Moormen who convey rice and salt from the sea coast on pack bullocks to the interior. Of this prosperity his dwelling gave abundant proof; for he had not only English crockery and cutlery, but a decanter mysteriously covered up with a floor mat, in which it was whispered wine was once seen. Two pictures in frames, in glaring colors, graced the walls, while on a kind of shelf was placed, by way of ornament, a jar with a faded gilt label, inscribed "leeches."

Not far removed from the constable in locality, and dignity of coffee, was the village peon and post holder, graceless and lazy as any within the Central Province of the Island, and that is saying a good deal: it would have been a difficult thing to have shown that Puncheyralle, the Post Holder did anything to entitle him to the name beyond bestowing an occasional kick on the letter carriers or runners as they passed through the village; yet the man grumbled at receiving no more than five rix-dollars or seven shillings and sixpence a month, for the discharge of these onerous duties. Puncheyralle had a rather bustling little wife, who did all the heavy work for him, except the kicking: the pigs, the garden, the fowls, all were in her charge, and while she and the very small children cooked the meals, and kept the house in order, their lord and master lay on his back, or beat the tom-tom or native drum, or perhaps gambled with a neighbour for a few copper challies.

The remainder of the village was made up of families generally poor enough, who derived their sole support from the produce of their patrimonial lands. In several instances the domestic arrangements of these people, with a view of keeping their little property from dwindling away by frequent divisions, were singular enough to an English mind. There were two or three households in which several brothers had but one wife amongst them,* and singular as this custom may appear to Europeans, they dwelt together most harmoniously: indeed family quarrels were at that time exceedingly rare.

A picture of one of these groups is a portrait of them all. Poor to abject misery in all but rice and a few fine grains, these people are invariably landholders, some of them on an infinitessimally small scale despite the marital arrangements I have mentioned. At times the family will be large, swelled by the addition of an aged grandfather or grandmother, or some such relation, and with, occasionally, a numerous progeny of all ages. Beyond the culture of their rice, of primary importance, the ground that produces their few additional necessaries such as chillies, tobacco and fine grain is little enough. A few of them possess one or two buffaloes; most of them have a caricature of a pig and a few scarecrows of fowls; but there is only one milch cow in the entire range of Malwattie.

It was truly astonishing to see how early the young children were put to tasks of strength. The boys were made to look after the buffaloes and the rice-fields, while the girls were set to weave mats, pound the rice from the husk, fetch water, and such work. Often have I seen a little delicate child, six or seven years of age, staggering up a tolerably steep path, with an infant placed astride accross its little hip, and a huge earthen chattie of water on its head. Such early toil as this,

---

* Since the date at which this was written (1852) Polygamy in the Kandyan country has been forbidden by legal enactment.

equally early marriage, and generally poor and scanty diet, lead to one inevitable result, premature old age.

The Priest made a pretence at keeping schoocl but I failed to learn the nature of the instruction he professed to give. A dozen dusky infants assembled within the porch of the Vihare occasionally, and there, squatted on the ground, chanted a dismal alphabetical chorus: but I never found any progress made beyond this preparatory arrangement.

There was but one exception to the sameness of the population of Malwattie; it consisted of a small household, not far from the foot of the hill near the Vihara, and closely adjoining the bullock-track or bridle path leading past my estate from the highroad. Here, beneath a pretty tope of neverfading trees, where blossom and fruit and sweetest perfumes played their part all through the year, dwelt a blind old man and his pretty grand-daughter. The tiny hut they dwelt in was not more diminutive than neat: so clean, and white and fresh within; without, all was beauty and order. Had a whole legion of mountain sylphs and wood-nymphs been busily employed about the place all night long and every day, it could not have been kept in more perfect and picturesque neatness. The little fence around the cottage was so nicely trimmed; the garden in front so well swept and watered; the orange and lime trees so carefully tended, and always so delighted to bear plenty of fruit for dear little Dochie to gather, that they did not bend and droop with the heavy clusters of golden wealth, as some trees would have done, but actually danced and leaped about in the morning and evening breezes, as though their burden were no burden but the merest pastime.

Pretty little Dochie, gentle little Dochie, was not more than twelve years of age when I first made her acquaintance, one hot morning in the dry season. I caught her gathering some oleander blossoms and roses, and country jessamine, and thought I had never seen anything half so lovely, barring her colour. I reined in my pony and asked her for a draught of water;

instead of looking alarmed, as would most of her class when

thus accosted, she smiled good-naturedly, and tripped into the little cottage. I was off my nag and in the pretty flower-garden when she came out with a cocoa-nut shell of—not water, but bless the dear child—rich, white, goat's milk. I am not quite sure, but I rather think I must have kissed her, as I returned her the homely flagon; at any rate, we became the best of friends, and it ended in Dochie taking me to see her old blind grandfather, who was busily working at a net of some sort, and then to inspect one of the neatest little farm-yards, I had ever seen out of old England. The whole place was a perfect miracle of industry and neatness; and I could not help asking how she managed to keep it so. It appeared that their neighbours assisted, at certain seasons, in working the garden and bringing it into good order, and that the old man helped her to carry the water from the little bamboo spout, which the villagers had fixed for them to convey a supply from the hill stream at some distance, to the extremity of their property.

They appeared to be in want of nothing that could make them comfortable; as to money, they had little enough, their sole earnings being from the sale of her goats' milk, flowers and fruit to wayside travellers. She assured me, that when the pilgrims passed on their way to the sacred foot-print on Adam's Peak, she sold as many flowers and as much fruit as the garden could produce, and enabled them to be quite extravagant in white cloths and handkerchiefs.

From that time forward I never passed through Malwattie without a draught of fresh milk and a little bouquet gathered by Dochie's own tiny hand. At length it came to my dismounting regularly, and in course of time, amongst other things we talked of, were books and knowledge. Her dark bright eyes sparkled as I told her what wonders she might learn if she could but read English books. The strange art was now her sole thought, and one day she found courage to ask me how she could learn it. I hesitated, for I did not quite see how to help her; but when I offered to send her a book with the English alphabet, and moreover, to teach her to read the letters, her joy was unbounded. In a few months, my pupil had not only mastered the alphabet, but could spell small words, and read several short sentences. Not content with this, I talked to her of religion, and explained the nature and history of Christianity as well as my ability allowed me. I was not quite so successful here; but I was content to pave the way for future labourers, and rejoiced to find her always anxious for truth.

It was, I think, quite a year after my first acquaintance with Dochie, that one morning I alighted as usual and was surprised to find my pupil absent, and in her place a young Cingalese man, evidently of the low country. My surprise was equalled by his own. In a minute after Dochie came bounding in with eggs and milk, and some little light cakes just prepared for the stranger, who, I then perceived, had his arm bandaged, and altogether looked fatigued and ill. I did not remain long that day; and learned, on retiring to mount my pony, that the stranger had sought refuge there very early that morning, having in vain begged through the village for a resting-place; he had been robbed and beaten during the previous night on some lonely track, and Dochie hesitated not one moment in welcoming him within their little dwelling; and, in her own singleness and purity of heart, acting the good Samaritan. I could but admire her kindness; and yet mixed with admiration, was a feeling akin to jealousy. I wished that it had been my fate to have been robbed and beaten, if only for the pleasure of being tended by the gentle Dochie.

Again months rolled on, the low-country stranger and the robbers were all forgotten. Changes had been, meanwhile, stealing over the face of the hitherto changeless Malwattie, and those not for the better. The worst of all innovations was the establishment of an arrack tavern in the very heart of the village. The Government in its anxiety to add to its revenue, and increase its means of developing the resources of the country, (I think that was what they termed it) had granted permission to the renter of the arrack licenses for the Kandyan country, to establish a few score additional taverns, one of which novelties was located in Malwattie; and soon where before had been quiet contentment, was nothing but brawling riot. It is true the Executive presented an antidote with the poison, by establishing a free school opposite the noisy tavern; but education stood small chance in competition with arrack, and for every new pupil at the desk there were a score of fresh drunkards. This led to an increase in the duties of the police, and soon after, to a salary to the head-constable; crime was on the increase; law suits were instituted; families at peace for several generations, became deadly enemies; and ere a year had elapsed since the introduction of the tavern, the whole social fabric of Malwattie was rent and disrupted into ugly fragments.

I continued to visit my friends the Korale and the Priest, both of whom, especially the latter, spoke bitterly of the arrack nuisance, and looked upon the establishment of the school as a direct attack upon Buddhism. I saw plainly however, that there was another and deeper feeling, antagonistic to the educational scheme, in the bosoms of these leading men of the place. They felt that by diffusing enlightenment amongst the poorest of the villagers, the British Government would in time raise the masses of the people above the level of the headmen, in which case their influence would at once disappear. Their unflinching opposition was but little needed, for the native cultivators could not be made to appreciate that knowledge which their immediate superiors did not possess. Too prone to take as their models those above them, the villagers were content to remain as they knew their fathers had been, and as they saw Korales and Dessaves were. Unfortunately, those in charge of Government schools have yet to learn that they have been toiling with the broad end of the educational wedge foremost; that in Eastern countries enlightenment can only flow downwards, never upwards: that to elevate the Indian serfs, you must first improve the intellectual capacities of those whom they ever have, and ever will regard as their patterns.

My progress with the flower-girl's schooling was satisfactory, and I had besides, the pleasure of finding her inclined to cast aside the superstitions of Buddha. In these tasks I was at this time aided by the teacher of the Government school, a Portuguese descendant, who seconded my efforts most zealously. The months flew rapidly past, and twice a week found me and Dochie seated beneath the shady foliage of a young orange tree, deep in our labors.

It was quite the end of the hot season, that I was compelled to leave my plantation and journey across the country to the opposite coast of the Indian peninsula, in search of Malabar labourers to secure the coming crop. I was absent nearly two months, and found myself one cool pleasant day in August riding homewards across the broad open prairie-lands adjoining Malwattie. The rich foliage of the jungle and the gardens shone as brightly as ever in the afternoon sun. The hill-streams rippled as pleasantly down their stony courses. Yet the village was no longer the spot I once knew it; brawling and angry words were easily met with; its old patriarchal peace and simplicity had departed from it. I rode on musingly, and at length pulled up in front of Dochie's little garden; I started in my saddle at observing that it also was changed, and so sadly too. The friendly orange tree with its yellow fruit and its pleasant shade, was not there. The oleanders were drooping in the ground; some of the fence was torn down, and a vile black bullock, that I could have massacred on the spot, was cruelly browsing over the flower-beds. The door was closed; the shutters were fastened. I imagined all sorts of calamities to have happened, everything in short but what was actually the case. I made one brief inspection of the new neglected place; then mounted my pony and rode homewards fearing lest some villager should break the tale of sorrow.

It was nearly evening when I rode up the winding path leading to my bungalow, oppressed with a fear of I knew not what. The old building stood, as it ever had done, quietly and humbly in the midst of the coffee fields, but I saw at once there were some changes. I could scarcely believe my eyes when I beheld in the centre of the little grass plot, facing my front verandah, some small flowering shrubs and an orange tree so like the one I had missed from Dotchie's garden that I began to fancy I was still down in the village, and that the little flower-girl was peeping at me from behind some of the coffee bushes.

As I stood looking at the orange tree my servant placed a letter in my hand, traced in true native style, on a dry leaf in Cingalese characters. It was from my pupil herself, and told me in a few simple sentences all that had occurred. I breathed more freely to find her alive. She was married, she said to a young and rich Cingalese trader, a christian and inhabitant of Colombo. She hoped shortly to be admitted a member of our Church, and thanked me deeply for what I had done for her. The old blind man her grandfather was with them, and they were all happy. They trusted I should always be so. In my garden, she said, she had caused to be planted the orange tree I had so often admired and sat under, with a few flowers from her garden. She prayed that for many years to come, the tree would yield me plentiful crops of cool, refreshing fruit.

The reader will perhaps smile when I say that, after reading this note, I shed some tears, tears of real sorrow and pain. Heaven knows I wished the poor girl well and happy; but though I never could have looked on her other than as a gentle innocent acquaintance, loveable for her simple purity, I felt her departure keenly. To the many dwellers in the thronged cities of the west, the loss of such a companion of my wild, lonely, jungle-life, may appear trivial enough ; yet to me it was an event.

My servant told me what the little note had omitted. Dochie had been wooed and won with true Cingalese brevity, by the same young low-countryman who had been so kindly sheltered and tended by her when robbed and beaten, as I have before told. He had been successful in trade, and had now a large store in Colombo.

It was long before I ventured again near Malwattie. To me it was no more a "garden of flowers" and least of all did I care to pass by the green fence and gate where Dochie's pretty smiling face had so often welcomed me. At last I persuaded the old Korale to set some of the villagers to work and open a new path for me nearer his own bungalow, by which means I ever after avoided a spot, the sight of which served but to fill me with vain regrets. The place and the people were so changed that I soon become a stranger in the village.

OUR COOK'S WEDDING.

IN some parts of the East, and especially in the Island of Ceylon, there are many old customs which the progress of civilization has not as yet effaced; and happily so, for they serve to keep up a kind and friendly feeling between the different classes and races of the country. One of these time-honoured customs is the presence of European or burgher employers at the weddings or family festivals of their native servants who seldom omit inviting their masters and families on such occasions. Being the guest of an old resident of Colombo, I received an invitation to be present at the nuptials of his head cook, a Cingalese of good ancestry, who it appeared was to be united to the ayah or waiting-maid of a neighbour. They were both Catholics; and, as such, were to be married at one of the churches with which the native section of the town abounds. From some cause, my host could not attend on the eventful day. I was, therefore, left to make my way alone to the happy scene, which I learnt lay at some distance from our bungalow, at the further end of the long straggling outskirts.

Noon was the appointed time; the Church of Saint Nicholas the place; and in order that I might examine the locality I was about to visit, and which was entirely new to me, I left my quarters soon after our breakfast of rice and curry. It was a truly tropical day: the sea-breeze had not commenced to blow, and the cool land-wind had been fairly done up an hour since. In mercy to the horse and the runner by his side, I ordered the man to drive slowly. The sky seemed hot and coppery—too warm to look blue; and the great orb of light and heat had a sort of lacquered hue that was oppressive in the extreme. Round the great lake, past the dry, stagnant, putrid fort-ditch, to that part of the Black Town known as Sea Street. How different from the quiet, broad Dutch streets, or the cool, shady lanes and their fine old burgher mansions! Here all was dust, and dirt, and heat. A dense crowd of people, of many of the nations of the East, was passing to and fro, not, as with us, along the pavement—for there was no footway—but horses, bullocks, carriages, donkeys, and human beings all hurried along pell-mell: Arabs, Moormen, Chinese, Parawas, Cingalese, Kandyans, Malays, Chitties, Parsees, and Bengalis, were jostling each other in strange confusion. I shuddered as I beheld a brace of overheated bullocks in an empty cart, rush madly past me into the midst of a whole host of men, women, and children; but, strange to tell, no one seemed any the worse: there was, to be sure, a little rubbing of shins, and a good deal of oriental swearing on the occasion, but no more. A vicious horse broke away from his Arab leader, and dashed across the street, and down a narrow turning, where women and children seemed to be literally paving the way; the furious animal bounded over and amongst the living pavement, knocking down children of tender years, and scattering elderly females right and left, but still harmlessly. I felt puzzled at this, and concluded that they were "used to it."

The thronged street, along which I was slowly travelling, appeared to be the only thoroughfare of any length, shape, or breadth. From it diverged, on all sides, hundreds of dwarf carriage-ways—turnings that had been lanes in their younger days. They were like the Maze at Hampton Court, done in mud and masonry. I have often heard of crack skaters cutting out their names upon the frozen Serpentine; and, as I peeped up some of these curious zigzag places, it seemed as though the builders had been actuated by a similar desire, and had managed to work their names and pedigrees in huts, and verandahs, and dwarf-walls. Into these strange quarters few, if any Europeans ever care to venture; the sights and the effluvia are such as they prefer avoiding, with the thermometer standing at boiling-point in the sun. Curiosity, however, got the better of my caution; and, descending from my vehicle, I leisurely strolled up one of those densely-packed neighbourhoods, much to the annoyance of my horsekeeper, who tried hard, in broken English, to dissuade me from the excursion. Whether it be that the native families multiply here more rapidly, in dark and foul places, I know not; but never had I seen so many thrown together in so small a space. Boys and girls abounded in every corner. As I passed up this hot, dusty, crooked lane of huts, the first burst of the cool sea-breeze came up from the beach, glowing with health and life. I looked to see how many doors and windows would be gladly flung open to catch the first of the westerly wind, and chase away the hot, damp, sickly air within; but I looked in vain. Not a door creaked on its rusty hinges, not a window relaxed its close hold of the frame; the glorious light of day was not to be permitted to shine upon the foul walls and floors of those wretched hovels.

There was business, however, going on here and there. The fisher and his boy were patching up an old worm-eaten canoe, ready for the morrow's toil; another son was hard at work upon the net that lay piled up in the little dirty verandah. Next door was a very small shoemaker, sharing the little front courtyard with a cooper, who did not appear to be working at anything in particular: but was rather disposed to soliloquize upon buckets and tubs in general, and to envy the hearty meal which a couple of crows were making of a dead rat in the street. Farther on was a larger building, but clearly on its last legs, for it was held up by numberless crutches. It was not considered safe to hold merchandise of any description; and, as the owner did not desire the trouble and expense of pulling it down, he had let it out to a Malay, who allowed strangers to sleep in it on payment of a small nightly fee. As

I passed by, a crowd of poor Malabars, just arrived from the opposite coast of India, were haggling for terms for a night's lodging for the party, and not without sundry misgivings; for some looked wistfully at the tottering walls, and pointed with violent gestures, to the many props.

Wending my slow way back towards the main street, I came upon a busy carpenter's shop—a perfect model of the kind. In this country some carpenters are also carriage-builders, and the place I then stopped to examine was the home of one of these. It was a long, low, rambling shed, such as we might consider good enough to hold cinders or firewood: the leaf-thatched roof had been patched in many places with tattered matting; the crazy posts were undermined by the pigs in the next yard, where they shared the dirt and the sun with a heap of wretched children, and a score of starving dogs. Every kind of conveyance that had been invented since the flood, appeared to have a damaged representative in that strange place. Children's shattered donkey-carriages, spavined old breaks, and rickety triacles of the Portugues period, hackeries of the early Malabar dynasty, palanquins of Cingalese descent, Dutch governors' carriages, English gigs, were all pent up, with irrecoverable cart-wheels, distorted carriage-poles, and consumptive springs. Had I possessed any antiquarian experience, I doubt not I should have discovered amongst the mass an Assyrian chariot or two, with a few Delhi howdahs. The master-mind of this coach-factory was a genuine Cingalese who, in company with a slender youth, was seated on his haunches upon the ground, chisel in hand, contemplating, but not working at a felly for some embryo vehicle. After one or two chips at the round block of wood between his feet, Jusey Appoo paused, arranged the circular comb in his hair, and took another mouthful of betel; then another chip at the wood; and then he rose, sauntered to the door, and looked very hard up the little lane and down it, as though ho momentarily expected some dreadful accident to happen to somebody's carriage in the next street.

Once more in my vehicle, I threaded the entire length of Sea Street, with its little dirty shops; the sickly-smelling arrack taverns; the quaint of old Hindu temple, bedecked with flowers and flags inside, and with dirt outside; and the whitewashed Catholic churches. Little bells were tinkling at these churches; huge gongs were booming forth their brazen thunder from the heathen temples; there was a devil-dance in one house to charm away some sickness, and a Jesuit in the next hovel confessing a dying man. There was a chorus of many tiny lungs at a Tamil school, chanting out their daily lessons in dreary verse, and a wilder, older chorus at the arrack-shop just over the way, without any pretence to time or tune. The screams of bullock-drivers; the shouts of horse-keepers; the vociferations of loaded coolies; the screeching of rusty cart-wheels begging to be greased; the din of the discordant checkoo or oil-mill;—all blended in one violent storm of sound, made me glad to hasten on my way, and leave the maddening chorus far behind. The open beach, with its tall fringe of graceful cocoa-palms, and its cool breeze, was doubly welcome. I was sorry when we left it, and drove slowly up a steep hill: on the summit of which stood the Church of St. Nicholas, my destination.

A busy scene was there. Long strings of curious-looking vehicles were ranged outside the tall white church—so white and shiny in the sun, that the bullocks in the hackeries dared not look up at it. I felt quite strange amongst all the motley throng: and when I stared about and beheld those many carts, and palanquins, and hackeries, I fancied myself back again in Jusey Appoo's coach-factory. But then these were all gaily painted, and some were actually varnished, and had red staring curtains, and clean white cushions, and radient little lamps. Nearer the church, were some half-a-dozen carriages, with horses, poor enough of their kind, but still horses with real tails. I glided in amongst the crowd, unnoticed, as I too fondly believed, and was about to take up a very humble position just inside one of the great folding-doors, when I was accosted by a lofty Cingalese in gold buttons and flowing robes, with a gigantic comb in his hair, and politely led away captive, I knew not whither. Down one side-aisle, and across a number of seats, and then up another long aisle ; and to my utter discomfiture, I found myself installed on the spot, in the unenviable post of a "Lion" of the day's proceedings. To a person of modest temperament, this was a most trying ordeal. There was not another white face there: Cookey had been disappointed, it seemed in his other patrons, and knowing of my intended visit, had waited for my appearance to capture me and thus add to the brilliancy of the scene.

I bowed to the bride, with as little appearance of uneasiness as I could manage ; but when I turned to the bridegroom, I had nearly forgotten my mortification in a burst of laughter. The tall uncouth fellow had exchanged his wonted not ungraceful drapery for a sort of long frock-coat of blue cloth, thickly bedecked with gay gilt buttons, and sham gold-lace: some kind of a broad belt of gaudy colour hung across his shoulders: he wore boots, evidently far too short for him, which made him walk in pain; and, to complete the absurdity of his attire, huge glittering rings covered half of his hands. The lady was oppressed with jewellery which, on these occasions, is let out on hire: she seemed unable to bend or turn for the mass of ornaments about her. White satin shoes and silk stockings gave a perfect finish to her bridal attire.

As the party marched up to the priest, I felt as a captive in chains gracing a Roman triumph. No one of all that crowd looked at the bride; they had evidently agreed among themselves to stare only at me. I felt that I was the bride, and the father, and the best man. I looked around once; and what a strange scene it was in the long white church! There were hundreds of black faces, all looking one way—at me—but I did not see their faces; I saw only their white eyes glistening in the bright noon-day sun, that came streaming through the great open windows, as though purposely to show me off. I wished it had been midnight. I hoped fervently that some of the hackery bullocks would break loose, and rush into the church, and clear me a way out. I know nothing of how the marriage was performed, or whether it was performed at all; I was thinking too much of making my escape. But in a very short time by the clock, though terrifically long to me, I found myself gracing the Roman triumph on my way out. The fresh air rather recovered me; and what with the drollery of handing the cook's wife into the cook's carriage, and the excitement of the busy scene, and the scrambling for hackeries, and the galloping about of unruly bullocks, I felt determined to finish the day's proceedings. I knew the worst.

I followed the happy couple in my vehicle, suceeded by a long line of miscellaneous conveyances, drawn by all sorts of animals. Away we went, at a splitting pace, knocking up the hot dust, and knocking down whole regiments of pigs and children. Up one hill, and down another, and round two or three rather sharp corners, as best our animals could carry us. At last there was a halt. I peeped out of my carriage, and found that we were before a gaily decorated and flower-festooned bungalow, of humble build: the house of the conjugal cook. Up drove all the bullock hackeries, and the gigs, and the carts, but no one offered to alight. Suddenly a host of people rushed out of the little house in the greatest possible haste. They brought out a long strip of white cloth, and at once placed it between the bride's carriage and the house, for her to walk upon. Still there was no move made from any of the carriages, and I began to feel rather warm. At length a native came forward from the verandah, gun in hand, I supposed to give the signal to alight. The man held it at arm's length turned away his head, as though admiring some of our carriages and "snap" went the flint; but in vain. Fresh priming was placed in the pan: the warrior once more admired our carriages, and again the "snap" was impotent. Somebody volunteered a pin for the touch-hole, another suggested more powder to the charge, whilst a third brought out a lighted stick. The pin and the extra charge were duly acted upon. The weapon was grasped: the carriages were admired more ardently than before: the firestick was applied to the priming, and an explosion of undoubted reality followed. The warrior was stretched on his back. Half the hackery bullocks started and plunged out of their trappings, while the other half bolted. To add to the dire confusion, my villainous steed began to back very rapidly towards a steep bank, on the edge of which stood a quiet, old-fashioned pony in a gig with two spruce natives seated in it. Before they could move away, my horse had backed into the ponychaise; and the last I saw of them at that time, was an indistinct and rather mixed view of the two white-robed youths and the old-fashioned pony and chaise performing various somersaults into the grass-swamp at the base of the bank.

Glad to escape from the contemplation of my misdeeds, I followed the bridal party into the little house. Slowly alighting from her vehicle the lady was received by a host of busy relations; some of whom commenced salaaming to her, some scattered showers of curiously cut fragments of coloured and gilt paper over her and her better half—probably intended to represent the seeds of their future chequered happiness and troubles; and then, by way of inducing the said seed to germinate, somebody sprinkled over the couple a copious down-pouring of rose-water. The little front verandah of the dwelling was completely hidden beneath a mass of decorations of flowers, fruits, and leaves, giving it at first sight the appearance of some place between a fairy bower and a Covent Garden fruit-stall. The living dark stream poured into the fairy bower, and rather threatened the floral arrangements outside: the door-way was quickly jammed up with the cook's nearest and dearest relatives of both sexes; while the second cousins and half-uncles and aunts blocked up the little trap-door of a window with their grizzly, grinning visages. The room we were in was not many feet square: calculated to hold, perhaps, a dozen persons in ordinary comfort; but, on this occasion, compelled to welcome within its festive mud-walls at least forty. A small oval table was in the centre; a dozen or so of curiously-shaped chairs were ranged about the sides, in the largest of which the bride was seated. The poor creature was evidently but ill at ease: so stiff and heavily-laden with ornaments. The bridegroom was invisible, and I felt bound to wait upon the lady in his absence. The little darkened cell was becoming fearfully hot: indistinct ideas of the Black Hole at Calcutta rose to my heated imagination. A feverish feeling crept over me, not a little enhanced by the oriental odours from things and persons about me. The breeze, when it did manage to squeeze itself in, brought with it the sickly perfume of the myriads of flowers and leaves outside. Upon the whole, the half hour or so which elapsed between our arrival and the repast, was a period of intense misery to me, and vast enjoyment to the cook's family circle. There was nothing to while away the hot minutes: I had to look alternately at the bride, the company, and the ceiling; the company stared at myself and the lady; while she, in her turn, looked at the floor, hard enough to penetrate through the bricks to the foundation below. In the first instance I had foolishly pictured the breakfast, or whatever the meal was to be, set forth upon some grassy spot in the rear of the premises, under the pleasant shade of palms and mangoe trees.

But the vulgar crowd must be kept off by walls; and the little oval table in the centre of the cabin was to receive the privileged few, and to shut out the unprivileged many.

Dishes reeking hot, and soup-tureens in a state of vapour, were passed into the room, over the heads of the mob; for, there was no forcing a way through them. A long pause, and then some more steaming dishes, and then another pause, and some rice-plates; and at last, struggling and battling amidst the army of relations, the bridegroom made his appearance—very hot and very shiny, evidently reeking from the kitchen. He had slipped on his blue cloth, many buttoned coat, and smiled at his wife and the assembled company as though he would have us believe he was quite cool and comfortable.

It devolved upon me to hand, or rather drag the bride to one end of the table; opposite to whom sat her culinary lord and master, as dignified, and important, as though his monthly income had been ten guineas instead of ten rix-dollars. I seated myself next to the lady of the hut, and resigned myself to my fate; escape was out of the question. Nothing short of fire, or the falling-in of the roof, could have saved me. Our rickety chairs were rendered firm and secure as the best London-made mahogany-seats, by the continuous unrelenting pressure of the dense mob behind and around us. The little room seemed built of faces; you might have danced a polka or a waltz on the heads of the company with perfect security. As for the window-trap, I could see nothing but bright shining eyes through it.

The covers were removed, as covers are intended to be; but, instead of curiously arranged and many coloured dishes of pure and unadulterated Cingalese cookery, as I had, in the early part of the day, fondly hoped, there appeared upon them a few overdone, dried up joints *a l' Anglaise;* a skinny, consumptive baked shoulder of mutton; a hard-looking boiled leg of a goat; a shrivelled spare-rib of beef; a turkey that might have died of jungle-fever; and a wooden kind of dry, lean ham, with sundry vegetables made up this sad and melancholy show. All my gastronomic hopes, so long cherished amidst that heated assemblage, vanished with the dish-covers, and left me a miserable and dejected being. Ten minutes previously, I had felt the pangs of wholesome hunger, and was prepared to do my utmost; at that moment, I only felt empty and sick. Could I have reached the many-buttoned cook, I might have been tempted to have done him some bodily harm; but I could not move. The host had the wretch of a turkey before him. Well up to the knife-and-fork exercise, he whipped off from the breast of the skinny bird two slices of the finest meat—the only really decent cuts about it—and then, pushing the dish on to his next neighbour, begged him to help himself. Of course, I had to attend to the hostess. I gave her a slice of the sinewy lean ham before me, with two legs of a native fowl, and began to think of an attempt upon the boiled mutton for myself; but there was no peace for me yet. The bride had never before used a knife and fork, and, in her desperate attempts to insert the latter into one of the fowl's legs, sent it with a bound into my waistcoat, accompanied by a shower of gravy, and a drizzling rain of melted butter and garlic. Feeling more resigned to my fate, I proceeded to cut up her ham and chicken, and then fancied the task was done; but not so. Her dress was so tight, the ornaments so encompassed her as with a suit of armour, that all her attempts to reach her mouth with her fork were abortive. To bend her arm was evidently impossible. Once, she managed to get a piece of ham as high as her chin; but it cost her violent fractures in several parts of her dress; so that I became alarmed for what might possibly happen, and begged her not to think of doing it again, offering to feed her myself. Feverish, thirsty, and weary as I felt at that table, I could scarcely suppress a smile when I found myself, spoon in hand, administering portions of food to the newly-made wife. Never having had, at that period of my existence, any experience in feeding babies, or other living creatures, I felt at first much embarrassed, somewhat as a man might feel who, only accustomed to shave himself, tries, for the first time in his life, to remove the beard of some friend in a public assembly. Fortunately for me, the lady was blessed with a rather capacious mouth; and, as I raised, tremblingly and in doubt, a pyramid of fowl, ham, and onions, upon the bowl of the Brittannia-metal spoon, my patient distended her jaws in a friendly and hopeful manner.

During my spoon performances I was much startled at hearing, close to our door, the loud report of several guns fired in quick succession. I imagined at first that the military had been called out to disperse the mob, but as nobody gave signs of any alarm or uneasiness, that could not have been the case; so I settled in my mind that the friends of the family were shooting some game for the evening's supper. All that I partook of at that bridal party was a small portion of very lean, dry beef, and some badly boiled potatoes, washed down by a draught of hard, sour beer. I essayed some of the pastry, for it had a bright and cheerful look, and was evidently very light. I took a mouthful of some description of sugared puff, light to the feel, and pleasant to look at, but in reality a most heartless deception—a sickly piece of deceit: it was evidently a composition of bean-flour, brown-sugar, stale eggs, and cocoanut oil; the latter, although bnrning very brilliantly in lamps, and serviceable as a dressing to hair, not being quite equal to lucca oil, when fried or baked. To swallow such an abomination was impossible, and, watching my opportunity, I contrived at length to convey my savoury mouthful beneath the table. This vile pastry was succeeded by a plentiful crop of fruit of all kinds, from pine-apples to dates. Hecatombs of oranges, pyramids of plantains, shoals of sour-sops, mounds of mangoes, to say nothing of alligator-pears, rhambatams, custard-apples, guavas, jamboes, and other fruit, as varied in name and taste, as in hue and form, graced that hitherto graceless board. I had marked for immediate destruction a brace of custard apples, and a glowing, corpulent alligator-pear, and was even on the point of securing them before attending to my dark neighbour, when a loud shout, followed by a confused hubbub, was heard outside in front. There was a cracking of whips, and a rattling of carriage-wheels, and altogether a huge commotion in the street, which at once put a stop to our dessert, and attracted attention from the inside to the exterior of the house. My spirits revived from zero to summer-heat, and thence up to blood-heat, when I learnt that the arrivals were a batch of "Europe gentlemen," friends of the cook's master, who had come just to have a passing peep at the bride and the fun. Their approach was made known by sundry exclamations in the English language, and a noise as of scuffling at the door. How our new friends were to get in, was a mystery to me: nor did the host appear to have any very distinct ideas upon the subject. He rose from his seat, and, with his mouth full of juicy pine-apple, ordered a way to be cleared for the "great masters;" but he might as well have requested his auditory to become suddenly invisible, or to pass out through the key-hole. There was no such thing as giving way: a few of the first-cousins grinned, and one or two maternal uncles coughed audibly, while the eyes of the distant relations at the window were glistening more intensely, and in greater numbers than ever. The stock of British patience, as I rather expected, was quickly exhausted, and in a minute or two I perceived near the door some white-faces, that were rather familiar to me at a certain regimental mess-table. Uncles and brothers-in-law were rapidly at a discount, and there appeared every prospect of mere connexions by marriage becoming relations by blood. Some giant of a native ventured upon the hazardous speculation of collaring an officer who was squeezing past him, and received a friendly and admonitory tap in return, which at once put him *hors de combat*. The cook, enraged at the rudeness of his countryman, dealt a shower of knocks amongst his family circle; the visitors stormed the approaches, and at last carried the covered way; Cingalese gentry struggled and pushed, and tried in vain to repel the invaders; the fair sex screamed, and tried to escape; the *melee* became general and furious. I gave my whole attention to the bride, who kept her seat in the utmost alarm; her husband was the centre of attraction to the combatants, and in the midst of a sort of "forlorn hope" of the native forces, the heavily loaded table was forced from its centre of gravity. Staggering and groaning beneath the united pressure from fruit and fighting, the wooden fabric reeled and tottered, and at last went toppling over, amidst a thunder-storm of vegetable productions. It was in vain I pulled at the unhappy bride, to save her; she was a doomed woman, and was swept away with the fruity flood. When I sought her amidst the wreck and confusion, I could only discover heaps of damaged oranges, sour-sops, and custard-apples, her white satin shoes, the Chinese fan, and the four silver meat-skewers. By dint of sundry excavations, the lady was fairly dug out of the ruins, and carried off by her female friends; the room was cleared of the rebellious Cingalese, and a resolution carried unanimously, that the meeting be adjourned to the compound or garden at the back. Under the pleasant shade of a tope of beautiful palms, we sat and partook of the remains of the feast. The relations, once more restored to good humour, amused themselves in their own fashion; preparing for the dancing, and festivity, and illuminations, that were to take place in the evening. Our own little party sat there until some time after sunset, and when we had seen the great cocoanut-shells, with their flaring wicks, lighted up, and the tom-toms begin to assemble, we deemed it prudent to retire and seek a wholesome meal with our friends.

COFFEE PLANTING IN THE OLDEN TIME.

Chapter I.

IN the month of September, 1840, I started from Kandy to visit a friend who was in charge of one of the new coffee clearings then in progress. I was accompanied by a young planter well acquainted with the country and the natives, and who had offered to act as my guide. The clearing was distant about twenty-five miles. The route we took since became famous for rebellion and martial law; and concerning which one of the largest blue books of any session had been concocted.

As there was in those days no Matale Coach, we mounted our horses a good hour before day-break so as to ensure getting over the most exposed part of our journey before the sun should have risen very high—an important matter for man and beast in tropical countries. Towards noon, we pulled up at a little bazaar, or native shop, and called for "Hoppers and Coffee." I felt that I could have eaten almost anything, and truly one needs such an appetite to get down the dreadful black-draught which the Cingalese remorselessly administer to travellers, under the name of coffee. A basin of turbid inky-looking fluid covered with a thick scum of broken particles of coffee, that require to be skimmed off with the finger: such was the beverage.

The sun was already rather high in the horizon when we found ourselves suddenly at a turn of the road in the midst of a "clearing." This was quite a novelty to me; so unlike anything one meets with in the low country or about the vicinity of Kandy. The clearing in question lay at an elevation of fully three thousand feet above the sea-level, whilst the attitude of Kandy is not more than seventeen hundred feet. I had never been on a hill estate, and the only notions formed by me respecting a plantation of coffee, were of continuous, undulating fields and gentle slopes. Here it was not difficult to imagine myself amongst the recesses of the Black Forest. Pile on pile of heavy dark jungle rose before my astonished sight looking like grim fortesses defending some hidden city of giants. The spot we had opened upon was at the entrance of a long valley of great width, on one side of which lay the young estate to which we were going. Before us were, as my companion informed me, fifty acres of felled jungle in wildest disorder; just as the monsters of the forest had fallen so they lay, heap on heap, crushed and splintered into ten thousand fragments. Fine brawny old fellows some of them; trees that had stood many a storm and thunder-peal, trees that had sheltered the wild elephant, the deer, and the buffaloe, lay there prostrated by a few inches of sharp steel. The "fall" had taken place a good week before, and the trees would be left in this state until the end of October, by which time they would be sufficiently dry for a good "burn." Struggling on from trunk to trunk, and leading our horses slowly between the huge rocks that lay thickly around, we at last got through the "fall," and came to a part of the forest where the heavy, quick click of mauy axes told us there was a working party busily employed. Before us a short distance in the jungle, were the swarthy compact figures of some score or two of low country Cingalese plying their small axes with a rapidity and precision that was truly marvellous. It made my eyes wink again, to see how quickly their sharp tools flew about, and how near some of them went to their neighbours' heads.

In the midst of these busy people I found my planting friend, superintending operations in full jungle costume. A sort of wicker helmet was on his head, covered with a long padded white cloth, which hung far down his back, like a baby's quilt. A shooting jacket and trousers of checked country cloth; immense leech-gaiters fitting close inside the roomy canvas boots; and a Chinese-paper umbrella, made up his singular attire.

To me it was a pretty, as well as a novel sight, to watch the felling work in progress. Two axe-men to small trees; three, and sometimes four, to larger ones: their little bright tools flung far back over their shoulders with a sharp flourish, and then, with a "whirr," dug in the heart of the tree, with such exactitude and in such excellent time, that the scores of axes flying about me seemed impelled by some mechanical contrivance, sounding but as one or two instruments. I observed that in no instance were the trees cut through, but each one was left with just sufficient of the stem intact to keep it upright; on looking around, I saw that there were hundreds of trees similarly treated. The ground on which we were standing was extremely steep and full of rocks, between which lay embedded rich veins of arable soil. Where this is the case, the masses of stone are not an objection; on the contrary they serve to keep the roots of the young coffee plants cool during the long dry season, and, in like manner prevent the light soil from being washed down the hill-side by heavy rains. My planter-friend assured me that if the trees were to be at once cut down, a few at a time, they would so encumber the ground as to render it impossible for the workmen to gain access to the adjoining trees, so thickly do they stand together, and so cumbersome are their heavy branches. In reply to my inquiry as to the method of bringing all these trees to the ground, I was desired to wait until the cutting on the hill-side was completed, and then I should see the operation finished.

The small axes rang out a merry chime—merrily to the planter's ear—but the death-knell of many a fine old forest tree. In half-an-hour the signal was made to halt, by blowing a conch shell: obeying the order of the superintendent, I hastened up the hill as fast as my legs would convey me, over rocks and streams halting at the top, as I saw the whole party do. Then they were ranged in order, axes in hand on the upper side of the topmost row of cut trees. I got out of their way, watching anxiously every movement. All being ready the manager sounded the conch sharply, two score voices raised a shout that made me start again; forty bright axes gleamed high in air, then sank deeply into as many trees, which at once yielded to the sharp steel, groaned heavily, waved their huge branches to and fro, like drowning giants, then toppled over, and fell with a stunning crash upon the trees below them. These having been cut through previously, offered no resistance, but followed the example of their upper neighbours, and fell booming on those beneath. In this way the work of destruction went rapidly on from row to row. Nothing was heard but groaning, cracking, crushing, and splintering; it was some little time before I got the sounds well out of my ears. At the time it appeared as though the whole of the forest-world about me was tumbling to pieces; only those fell, however which had been cut, and of such not one was left standing. There they would lie after lopping off the principal branches until sufficiently dry for the torch that would blacken their massive trunks, and calcine their many branches into dusty heaps of alkali.

By the time this was completed, and the men put on to a fresh "cut," we were ready for our mid-day meal, the planters' breakfast. Away we toiled towards the Bungalow. Passing through a few acres of standing forest, and over a stream, we came to a small cleared space well sheltered from wind, and quite snug in every respect. It was thickly sown with what at a distance I imagined to be young lettuces, or, perhaps, very juvenile cabbage-plants, but I was told this was the "nursery," and those tiny green things were young Coffee plants with which it was intended to form the future Soolookande Estate. On learning that we had reached the "Bungalow," I looked about me to discover its locality, but in vain; there was no building to be seen; but presently my host pointed out to me what I had not noticed before—a small, low-roofed, thatched place, close under a projecting rock, and half hid by thorny creepers. I imagined this to be his fowl-house, or, perhaps, a receptacle for tools, but was not a little astonished when I saw my friends beckon me on, and enter at the low, dark door. This miserable little cabin could not have been more than twelve feet long by about six feet wide, and as high at the walls. This small space was lessened by heaps of tools, coils of string for "lining" the ground before planting, sundry boxes and baskets, an old rickety table, and one chair. At the farther end, if anything could be far in that hole, was a jungle bedstead formed by driving green stakes in the floor and walls, and stretching rope across them. I could not help expressing astonishment at the miserable quarters provided for one who had so important a charge, and such costly outlay to make. My host however, treated the matter very philosophically. Everything, he observed, is good or bad by comparison; and wretched as the accommodation appeared to me who had been accustomed to the large, airy houses of Colombo, he seemed to be quite satisfied; indeed, he told me, that when he had finished putting up this little crib, had moved in his one table and chair, and was seated, cigar in mouth, inside the still damp mud walls, he thought himself the happiest of mortals. I felt somewhat curious to know where he had dwelt previous to the erection of this unique building,—whether he had perched up in the forest trees or in holes in the rocks, as I had heard was done by the wild Veddahs of Bintenna.

I was told that his first habitation when commencing work up there, was suspended over my head. I looked up to the dark dusty roof, and perceived a bundle of what I conceived to be old dirty brown paper, or parchment-skin. Perciving my utter ignorance of the arrangement, he took down the roll, and spread it open outside the door. It turned out to be two or three huge Talipot leaves which he assured me was the only shelter he had possessed for nearly three months, and that too, during the rainy season. They might have measured ten feet in length, and possibly five in width; pretty well for a leaf or two: they were used by fastening a stout pole lengthways to two stakes driven in the ground; the leaves were hung across this ridge-pole mid-way, and the corners of them made fast by cords: common mats being hung at each end and under the leafy roof.

The "Lines," a long row of mud huts for the coolies, appeared to be much more comfortable than their master's dwelling. But this is necessarily the case, for unless they be well cared for they will not remain on a remote estate, such as this one was then considered. The first thing a good planter sees to is a roomy and dry set of "Lines" for the people: then the "Nursery" of coffee plants, and thirdly, a hut for himself.

The Superintendent assured me that none but those who had opened an estate in a remote district, could form any idea of the difficulties and privations encountered by the planter. "Folks may grumble as they like, down in Colombo, or in England," said my friend, "about the high salaries paid to managers, but if some of them had only a month of it up here, in the rains, I suspect they'd change their notions."

He had had the greatest difficuly at first in keeping but a dozen men on the place to clear ground for lines and nurseries: so strong is the objection felt by Malabars to new and distant plantations. On one occasion he had been quite deserted: even his old cook ran away, and he found himself with only a little Cingalese boy, aud his rice, biscuit and dried fish all but exhausted. As for meat, he had not tasted any for many days. There was no help for it he saw, but to send off the little boy to the nearest village, with a rupee, to buy some food, and try to persuade some of the village people to come up and assist him. When evening came on, there was no boy back, and the lonely planter had no fire to boil his rice. Night came on, and still he was alone: hungry, cold, and desolate. It was a Sabbath evening, and he pointed out to me the large. stone on which he had sat down to think of his friends in the old country; the recollection of his distance from them and of his then desolate Crusoe-like position, came so sadly, so bitterly upon him that the strong man wept like a child. I almost fancied I saw a tear start to his large eye, as he related the circumstance.

During that same night, as he lay sleeping supperless, fatigue having overcome hunger, a great storm of rain and wind arose, and far into the night he was rudely awoke by a sensation of intense cold: looking upwards from his jungle couch he saw a few stars twinkling between the flying masses of clouds, the rain falling on him as he lay. A strong gust of wind had swept away the talipot roof, and he had no resource but to creep in beneath his wretched stick bed, and lay shivering there until the cold morning broke.

Ceylon planters are proverbially hospitable: the utmost stranger is at all times sure of a hearty welcome for himself and his horse. On this occasion, my jungle friend turned out the best cheer his small store afforded. It is true, we had but one chair amongst us, but that only served to give us amusement in making seats of baskets, boxes, and old books. A dish of rice, and curry, made of dry salt fish, two red herrings, and the only fowl on the estate, formed our meal; and poor as the repast may appear to those who have never done a good day's journey in the jungles of Ceylon, I can vouch for the keen relish with which we all partook of it.

In the afternoon we strolled out to inspect the first piece of planting on the Soolookande estate. It was in extent about sixty acres, divided into fields of ten acres by narrow belts of tall trees. This precaution was adopted, I learnt, with a view to protect the young plants from the violence of the wind, which at times rushes over the mountains with terrific fury.

Unless thus sheltered by belts or by "staking," the young plants get loosened, or are whirled round until the outer bark becomes worn away, and then they sicken and die, or if they live, yield no fruit. "Staking" is simply driving a stout peg in the ground, and fastening the plant steadily to it, but it is an expensive process, The young trees in these fields had been put out during the previous rains of July, and though still very small, looked fresh and healthy. I had always imagined planting out to be a very simple and easy affair; but I now learnt that exceeding care and skill are required in the operation. The holes to receive the young coffee plant must be wide and deep; they can scarcely be too large, the earth must be kept well about the roots of the seedling in removing it; and care must be taken that the tap-root be neither bent, nor planted over any stone or other hard substance: neglect of these important points is fatal to the prosperity of the estate. The yellow drooping leaves, and stunted growth, soon tell the proprietor that his superintendent has done his work carelessly; but alas! it is then too late to apply any remedy, save that of replanting the ground.

I left this estate impressed with very different notions concerning the life and trials of a planter in the jungle from what I had gathered from mere Colombo gossip; and I felt that superintendents were not at all overpaid for their skill, patience, privations, and hard work.

Chapter II.

Having seen almost the commencement of the Sooloo-kande Coffee Estate, I felt a strong desire towards the end of the year 1846, to pay it a second visit, while in its full vigour. I wished to satisfy myself as to the correctness of the many reports. I had heard of its heavy crops, of its fine condition, its excellent work, and not least, of the good management during crop-time. My old acquaintance was no longer in charge; he had been supplanted by a stranger. However, I went armed with a letter from the Colombo agents, which would ensure more attention than was comprised in providing a bed and a meal.

I journeyed this time by another and rather shorter route. Instead of taking the Matelle road, I struck off to the right, past Davy's Tree, celebrated as the scene of the massacre of a large body of British officers and troops by the treacherous Kandians; and crossing the Mahavilla Ganga at Davy's Ferry, made the best of my way across the beautiful vale of Dombera, and thence towards the long range of mountains forming one flank of the Kallibokke valley. At the period of my former excursion this long tract of fertile country was one unbroken mass of heavy jungle: now, a dozen large estates, with bungalows and extensive works, were to be seen, enlivening the journey, and affording a mnch readier passage for the horsemen; for wherever plantations are formed good jungle paths are sure to be made. The ride was a most interesting one; mile upon mile of coffee lay before and around me, in various stages of growth—from the young seedling just put out, to the full-bearing bush, as heavily laden with red ripe coffee berries as any currant-bush in England with its fruit.

It was then the middle of November, and the very height of the planters' harvest. All appeared busy as I rode along, gathering on the old properties; weeding and "supplying" or filling up failures on the young estates. I halted but once for a cup of good wholesome coffee, and gladly pushed on, so as to reach my destination in good time for breakfast.

The many lovely prospects opening before me caused some little delay in admiration of the views; and, by the time I had ridden through the last piece of jungle, and pulled up at the upper boundary of "Soolookande," the forenoon was well advanced. The sun was blazing high above me, but its rays were tempered by a cool breeze that swept down upon me from the neighbouring mountain tops. The prospect from that lofty eminence was lovely in the extreme: steep ridges of coffee extended in all directions, bounded by piles of massive forest; white spots, here and there told of bungalows and stores; a tiny cataract rushed down some cleft rock, on one side; on the other a rippling stream ran gently along, thickly studded with water-cresses. Before me in the far distance, lay outstretched, like a picture scroll, the Matelle district, with its paddy fields, its villages, and its Vihares skirted by a ridge of mountains and terminated by the Cave Rocks of Dambool. At my feet, far below, lay the estate, bungalow, and works, and to them I made my way by a narrow and very steep bridle-path. So precipitous was the land just here that I felt rather nervous on looking down at the white buildings. The pathway, for a great length, was bordered by rose-bushes, in fullest blossom, perfuming the air most fragrantly; as I approached the bungalow, other flowering shrubs and plants were mingled with them, and in such excellent order was everything there that the place appeared to me more like a magnified garden than an estate. How changed since my former visit! I could scarcely recognise it as the same property. The bungalow was an imposing looking building, the very picture of neatness and comfort. How different to the old Talipot-leaf and the dirty little mud hut! The box of a place I had slept in six years before, would have stood easily in the dining room of this bungalow. A wide verandah surrounded the building, the white pillars of which were polished like marble. The windows were more like doors; and, as for the doors, one may speak of them as lawyers do of Acts of Parliament: it would be easy to drive a coach-and-six through them. The superintendent was a most gentlemanly man, and so was his Bengalee servant. The curry was delightfully hot; the water was deliciously cool. The chairs were like sofas; and so exquisitely comfortable after my long ride, that, when my host rose and suggested a walk down to the works, I regretted that I had said anything about them, and had half a mind to pretend to be too weary for a walk.

The store was a spacious, zinc-roofed building: it was boarded below, but the sides upwards were merely stout rails, for ensuring a thorough circulation of air through the interior. It presented a most busy appearance. Many strings of Malabar coolies were flocking in, along narrow paths, from all sides, carrying bags on their heads, filled with the ripe coffee. These had to pass in at one particular door of the store, into the receiving-floor, in the upper part of the building. A cangany was stationed there to see each man's gathering fairly measured; and to give a little tin ticket for every bushel, on the production of which the coolies were paid at the end of the month. Many coolies had their wives and children to assist them in the field, and these brought home very heavy bags of coffee likewise.

Passing on to the floor where the measuring was in progress, I saw immense heaps of ripe, cherry-looking fruit waiting to be passed below to the pulpers. All this enormous pile must be disposed of before the morning, or it will not be fit for operating on, and might be damaged. I saw quantities of it already gliding downwards, through little openings in the floor, under which I could hear the noise of some machinery in rapid motion, but giving out sounds like sausage machines in full "chop." Following my guide, I descended a ladder, between some ugly-looking wheels and shafting, and landed safely on the floor of the pulping room. "Pulping" is the operation of removing the outer husk, or "cherry," which encloses the parchment-looking skin containing a pair of coffee beans. This is performed by a machine called a pulper. It is a stout wooden or iron frame, supporting a fly-wheel and barrel of wood covered with sheet copper, perforated coarsely outwards, very like a huge nutmeg-grater. The barrel is made to revolve rapidly, nearly in contact with two chocks of wood. The coffee in the cherry being fed on to this by a hopper, is forced between the perforated barrel and the chocks; the projecting copper points tear off the soft cherry whilst the coffee beans, in their parchment case, fall through the chocks into the large box. These pulpers (four in number) were worked by a waterwheel of great power, and turned out in six hours as much coffee as was gathered by three hundred men during the whole day.

From the pulper box the parchment coffee is carried along channels by water to the cisterns, enormous square wooden vats. In these the pulped coffee is placed, just covered with water, in which state it is left for periods varying from twelve to eighteen hours, according to the judgment of the manager. The object of this soaking is to produce a slight fermentation of the mucilaginous matter adhering to the "parchment," in order to facilitate its removal, as otherwise it would harden the skin, and render the coffee very difficult to peel or clean. When I inspected the works on Soolookande, several cisterns of fermented coffee were being turned out to admit other parcels from the pulper, and also to enable the soaked coffee to be washed, coolies were busily employed shovelling the beans from one cistern to another; others were letting in clean water. Some were busy stirring the contents of the cisterns briskly about; whilst some, again, were letting off the foul water; and a few were engaged in raking the thoroughly-washed coffee from the washing platforms to the barbacues.

The barbacues on this property were very extensive;—about twenty thousand square feet, all gently sloped away from their centres, and smooth as glass. They were of stone coated over with lime, well polished, and so white, that it was with difficulty I could look at them with the sun shining full upon their bright surfaces. Over these drying grounds the coffee, when quite clean and white, is spread, at first thickly, but gradually more thinly. Four days' sunning are usually required, though occasionally many more are necessary before the coffee can be heaped away in the store without risk of spoiling: all that is required is to dry it sufficiently for transport to Kandy, and thence to Colombo, where it undergoes a final curing previous to having its parchment skin removed, and the faulty and broken berries picked out. Scarcely any estates are enabled to effectually dry their crops, owing to the long continuance of wet weather on the hills.

The "dry floor" of this store resembled very much the inside of a malting house. It was nicely boarded, and nearly half full of coffee, white and in various stages of dryness. Some of it, at one end, was being measured into two bushel bags tied up, marked and entered in the "packed" book, ready for despatch to Kandy. Everything was done on a system; the bags were piled up in tens; and the loose coffee was kept in heaps of fixed quantities as a check on the measuring. Bags, rakes, measures, twine, all had their proper places, allotted them. Each day's work must be finished off-hand at once; no putting off until to-morrow can be allowed, or confusion and loss will be the consequence. Any heaps of half dried coffee, permitted to remain unturned in the store, or not exposed on the "barbecue," will heat, and become discoloured and in that condition is known amongst commercial men as "country damaged."

The constant ventilation of a coffee store is of primary importance in checking any tendency to fermentation in the uncured beans; an ingenious planter has recently availed himself of this fact, and invented an apparatus which forces an unbroken current of dry warm air, through the piles of damp coffee, thus continuing the curing process in the midst of the most rainy weather.

When a considerable portion of the gathering is completed, the manager has to see to his means of transport, before his store is too crowded. A well conducted plantation will have its own cattle to assist in conveying the crop to Kandy; it will have roomy and dry cattle-pens, fields of guinea grass, and pasture grounds attached, as well as a manure pit into which all refuse and the husks of the coffee are thrown, to be afterwards turned to valuable account.

The carriage of coffee into Kandy is performed by pack-bullocks and sometimes by the coolies, who carry it on their heads, but these latter can seldom be employed away from picking during the crop time. By either means, however, transport forms a serious item in the expenses of a good many estates. From some of the distant plantations possessing no cattle, and with indifferent jungle paths, the conveyance of their crops to Kandy will often cost fully six shillings the hundred weight of clean coffee, equal to about three pence per mile. From Kandy to Colombo by the common bullock-cart of the country the cost will amount to two or three shillings the clean hundred weight, in all, eight or nine shillings the hundred weight from the plantation to the port of shipment, being twice as much for conveying it less than a hundred miles as it costs for freight to England, about sixteen thousand miles.* One would imagine that it would not require much sagacity to discern that, in such a country as this a railroad would be an incalculable benefit to the whole community. To make this apparent even to the meanest Cingalese capacity, we may mention that, at this present time,† transit is required from the interior of the island to its seaports for enough coffee for shipment to Great Britain alone, to make a railroad remunerative. What additional quantities are required for the especially coffee drinking nations which lie between Ceylon and the mother country, surpasses all present calculation; enough however is carried away from this island in the course of every year, the transit of which to its seaboard, would pay for a net-work of railways.

---

* By sailing ship *via* the Cape.

† 1846.

DUTCH COLOMBO.

ONCE upon a time when good Queen Bess reviewed her trusty troops at the Fort at Tilbury and sent her gallant fleet to meet the great Armada, the countrymen of Pedro Lopez manned many guns on the Colombo ramparts, and the flag of Portugal floated jauntily over each gateway. Where now is the Fort stood then the Citadel, or inner fortress: the outer walls of cabook and lime, armed with small brass guns, extended along much of what is Norris' Road as far as Saint John's river, then a veritable stream running from a portion of the lake to the sea: this outer wall stretched along its bank and terminated at the sea beach. Kayman's Gate and its tower being then a guarded approach from the open country, where the wooded hills of Wolfendhal and Hultsdorf in the distance, were often infested by troops of the King of Cotta in wily ambuscade.

The Dutch changed much of this, and though they did their utmost to live at peace with the Native sovereigns, spared no pains or cost to render their strong-hold impregnable. Forts were constructed at Hangwella, Panebakere, Mutwall, &c. The outer walls of Colombo along the river banks of Saint John, were demolished: the swamp round the Fort was excavated and converted into the present lake, the earth removed from it going to form Slave Island and a portion of the ramparts. At the same time the late Fort of Colombo was rebuilt on a larger scale and on scientific principles, and it is supposed must have occupied a quarter of a century in construction. The strength that was gained by these means and the more pacific policy of the Dutch, gave an amount of security to their possessions which ultimately emboldened their principal officers and a few of the civilians, to build houses at some distance in the country, at Hultsdorf, Grand Pass and Mattacooly on the banks of the Kelani. At the happy period of which I write, Proctors had not been invented: trade was in the hands of the government, and comprised little else than cinnamon and pepper.

Colpetty existed but as a native suburb: Mutwall and Grand Pass were open country, dotted about by a few Dutch villas, whilst the Pettah consisted of a number of pretty streets pleasantly shaded by soorya trees, the houses tenanted by families the heads of which occupied responsible posts nnder the government. No native trader had then desecrated by his half-nude presence, the mauy, well-kept rows of pleasant cheery dwellings.

In the days to which these pages refer, communication with Europe was carried on twice in each year, when the spring and autumn fleets left Holland for Ceylon, laden with the goods suited to tropical countries. Transported in the spirit to those bye-gone days, let us stand upon the Battenburg bastion and look out to sea with the Port Master and his chief pilot Jansz. The morning is bright, the air is cool and crisp, fresh from Adam's Peak, and the flag of the Dutch republic floats from the mast-head on the lofty outworks erected by the wave washed rocks where once stood a Chapel to the Blessed Virgin. The Chapel and the tower have long since disappeared, and the massive rock on which they were erected is now partially levelled on the verge of the old Galle Buck. Between those outworks and the fort walls the Port-Master dwelt, and they say a prettier house was not to be seen in all Dutch Colombo, nor a neater garden, or greener sward on which, on moonlight nights, Dutch maids and lads met to do honor to the host's hospitality, when was tapped for old citizens, many a store of ripe scheidam or may be well vatted arrack.

A sail, a sail! The signal is run up to the mast head, and quickly a gun is fired from the Commandant's quarters to awaken all those who may perchance be still asleep or dozing through the early morning. Yes, it is the spring fleet arrived, just in time for Christmas! And it is well, for stocks of all kinds are low, and even his Excellency has been compelled to use Kandyan tobacco and Caltura arrack in the place of the veritable articles from Holland. In less time than it would take to smoke a pipe of the true Virginian weed, the fort walls are crowded with soldiers, civilians and native followers, all anxious to see the three ships that are freighted with things as dear to the colonists almost as life. On they come lazily, their big sails flapping listlessly in the faint morning breeze, until the roads are reached, anchors are dropped, and ropes are coiled.

What a rush there is on shore to be sure; burly Dutch officials accustomed to doze away their lives under the sooriya trees before their offices, are on the move: troops are on the march; the Lascoryn guard are turned out with the proverbial band of tom-toms and reedy, shrieking pipes, and away they go past the Justice Hall which at that time stood facing the esplanade, just where the Council Chamber, Audit Office and other public buildings now look out across the sea-walls. The present fort Church of St. Peter's was then the Governor's house, with many reception rooms and a great audience hall. On they march round the esplanade extending partly over the site of the present Government house, and midway on which stood the fine old Dutch Church now levelled to the ground and gone, and on through the water-gate to the landing jetty where they draw up alongside the military guard assembled to do honor to the Commander of the squadron and the official new-comers.

A goodly crowd gathers about the landing place, and when the three boats from the squadron pull alongside the jetty, the guard presenting arms, and the Commander and his fellow captains with a supercargo and a few passengers of both sexes, step upon the soil of Ceylon, there is a great commotion and much interchange of salutations. Away the travellers are whirled in several unweildly conveyances of which there are no specimens in the present day, not even in the Museum. Do they drive to the Commandant's to report their arrival, to the Governor's to pay their respects? To neither of these, but to the Church on the esplanade, their first act on landing being to return thanks for a safe and happy arrival at their destination. The church in which this offering-up of thanks was made, is standing no longer. Demolished on the capture of the fort by the British, a portion alone remained standing until the year 1860, when, after having served as a powder magazine and then an ice house, it was finally razed to the ground, its site forming part of the esplanade. It stood at the south-west corner of the public green, close by where a wicket still opens on the old Galle Buck,

The thanksgiving service over, the Captains proceed to the Commandant's quarters to report their arrival, which is done over a few pipes of veritable Viriginia produced in great triumph by the skippers: that ceremony of Dutch good fellowship being terminated, the party proceed to the Governor's palace, a rare old building of such capacity that a Dutch regiment could be drilled and put through its manœuvres in the public reception room, now the body of St. Peter's: as for the audience hall and dining rooms, you could drive a carriage and four round it with the most perfect ease with plenty of room for the frisky leaders. Credentials are soon presented, and the new officials who have arrived by the fleet, are introduced and welcomed by Mynheer Van Somebody. This ceremonial over the party retire to the capacious verandah in the rear, looking out upon a terrace of rare breadth leading down to prettily laid out walks above a huge tank of water, where in modern times there flourished a garden, which later still has degenerated into a collection of carriage sheds and horses' stables at the service of government officials, though some of the fine old trees remain living, monuments of the Dutch Governor's rule.

Under a massive tamarind tree were ranged many seats and small tables; and here in the cool evening His Highness the Governor, and his chief officers were wont to find solace in pipes and schiedam, after the heated labor of the day. To this favorite spot the new arrivals were conducted, the ladies from the fleet being consigned to the Governor's wife and her family. Need it be said how earnestly the news of old fatherland, of friends at home, of many long forgotten folk were listened to, and how doubly welcome to the half-starved-out officials were some stout flagons of the best Hollands and a portly packet of fragrant Virginia. How the flavor of those importations gave new zest to the guests' recitals of home events, and how vast clouds of smoke rose and disported themselves amidst the wide branches of the tamarind tree above, until supper was announced, when the guests followed the slow steps of mine host towards the great refectory hall where ponderous tables bore generous fare for all comers.

Not only the high officials grow merry on this red-letter day for all Colombo, but citizens of every degree,—the lower officials, the troops, the military and civil underlings have all reason for rejoicing, now that the spring fleet has come, and brought letters from friends and good cheer for every body. Beer Street, now known as Chatham Street, is alive with mirth and music: there is dancing and revelry within every other house: a corner building with huge gables, looking out upon the fort canal, where now a British wine merchant holds goodly stocks of costly liquors, a merry motley party chiefly of under civilians were entertained by the Captain of the Burghers. The evening meal being over, the tables were moved aside and to the sound of mirth-provoking music the whole party joined in the frantic movements of the Ceylon "Caffreina," a kind of tropical "Cancan," in vogue to the present time. It is a dance admitting of considerable latitude in regard to the movements of legs and arms; and it may be said of the head too, and one might almost marvel how it came to pass that a dance of such vigorous vitality could possibly find favor in any country, so near the equatorial line as Ceylon, especially in a Dutch colony;

but it was a dance not pertaining so much to Hollanders as to old Portugese colonists who cherished it and went in for it on every permissable occasion. Nevertheless it is a dance admitting of much grace and pleasing effect when accompanied by moderately slow and not wildly frantic music: the gently sweeping undulations of a proficient in the Caffreina are as pleasing and far more graceful than many modern drawing-room dances.

There are other and quieter little parties coming off in various parts of the Fort. Away beneath the Battenburg bastion for instance, the Port Master, Van Cuylenberg, is entertaining a goodly gathering of friends on the green before his pretty little Villa, where sooriya trees have been many years struggling for a crooked and at times doubtful existence against their dire enemy, the salt sea wind. But there they are, good-natured looking, humpbacked dwarfs, ready to extend a friendly branch to any young lad or maiden seeking for a seat on the soft sandy sward beneath. On the night on which this "Toddy Party" was held a good many lads and maidens were accommodated by their steady friends, the sooriyas, some of whose straggling branches descended so low as to form veritable bowers within which goodness only knows what may have occurred in matters of flirting. On an open space away from the sly sooriyas, were placed small, round, big-legged ponderous tables up to any weight of cakes and toddy jugs. Oh, those jolly jugs of brown ware, of real Haarlem make, but filled with sweet toddy-cup of Lanka! How they leered out upon the assembled guests as though to coax the young maidens from their snug hiding-places. How proudly the portly cakes oozing with luscious ghee and saccharine substances, peered down from their lofty vantage ground upon the humble "hoppahs" that lay pell-mell on wide delft platters, looking as abashed at their flat insignificance as though hoping to be soon devoured and hid from sight.

But bless us, long before the good dame Van Cuylenberg and the widow Plaats, and the elderly spinsters, the Van Graafs, had half finished their critical essay on the dress and the deportment of the female new comers, such games, such rompings were a-foot in the moonlight, that must have driven a cynical old on-looker bachelor like Van Graafs, the "powder master," mad with envy. But even the nimble-footed Laura, the agile Lydia, must yield in time, from frolicsome wearyness and as pretty dimple-faced Laura positively refused then and there, to dance the Caffreina, there was nothing for it but to take to creature comforts, and so it came to pass that a great and happy gathering was seen around those dumpy, ponderous tables whose loads of hoppahs and cakes, whose jugs of toddy-cup rapidly became small by degrees and beautifully less, until the wise ones of the party gave the signal for dispersing, and all made their happy way to pleasant homes not far away, to dream of the bright and gorgeous things the fleet had brought at that gay Christmas-tide.

OUR OLD CLERK.

THE air about the old fort walls in the old fort streets was still and steamy. Not a leaf or a twig on the Sooriya trees, would have moved for love or money. The sky looked as though it had been black leaded, and polished for the new monsoon that was making itself heard in the distance, far out at sea,—perspiring sparrows deserted the hot house-tops,—crows forgot to "caw," so stifling was the weather in that sultry month of May.

In a large, rambling, corner-house, near the south gate, wherein the last King of Kandy had been confined a state prisoner before embarking on his Indian exile, things went on as quietly as though a crisp land-wind were drifting through the cool gloomy offices. Our old clerk was placidity personified, as calm and self-possessed as in his prime, and yet the idea of having to make over the custody of the journal and ledger, to a young English lad, as I then was, cannot have been altogether agreeable to old Samuel's pride of place. But there was no help for it: the business of the firm had increased, the faithful chief clerk was growing aged apace, and it was found no longer possible for him to fulfil the many multifarious duties, hitherto entrusted to him, so implicitly and so successfully.

Samuel had been prepared for the change, and now when the time was come, when he was to know the Firm's ledger no longer, he put a bold face on it, and made a Dutch virtue of an English necessity. Before inducting me, he looked me well over, from head to foot, smiled half encouragingly, half compassionately, as though he would say "you don't know the weighty responsibility there is in that ledger," and then, taking the ponderous, strong-backed volume from an iron safe, large and massive enough to have been some firm's strong room, placed it before me, wiping it carefully and delicately with his pocket-handkerchief. Had the ancient Samuel been bestowing his eldest daughter upon me in marriage, he could not have shewn more anxiety about my reception and treatment of the precious charge entrusted to my custody. No horse-dealer could have taken more pains to indicate the rare points of a steed, than did the old clerk, to point out the beauties of his ledger,—*his* alas, no longer.

Samuel was a Dutchman, as much as his father and his grand-father: his mother was just as Dutch: and yet how different to Knickerbocker's Dutchmen, or the dwellers on the muddy banks of the Zuyder Zee. There was no ponderous mellow frame, encased loosely in baggy trousers of any size. No slouch hat, no long Dutch pipe: Samuel was slim, slight and dry as his own snuff-box. A beautifully fitting, snow-white jacket, and a yellow waistcoat, and nankeen trousers, full with many pleats round the waist, and a vast cavern of a pocket in which was hidden away a cambrick handkerchief of such marvellous dimensions, that one might have taken it to be the youngest baby's sheet. Thin shoes and white cotton socks, and above all a ponderous silver watch and massive gold chain, made up his Indian Dutch exterior.

He was the Firm's confidential clerk, but he was a good deal more than that: he was their chief negotiator and adviser in all delicate treatise with obstinate native traders who naturally wished to have all the bargains arranged after their own indigenous way. He was the great ratifier of difficult contracts for produce, or obstinate sales in the matter of wares from Manchester, Sheffield, or Glasgow. He was the presiding genius of the godowns, in which were stored and sorted, and packed, rich spices and fragrant seeds, and valuable Coffee; he was a sort of Hollando-oriental Simon-the-Cellarer, in whose custody were wonderful casks, and corpulent, strong-hooped vats, and curious bottles in dark, cobwebby corners full of rat holes: he was the Plutus of the establishment, in whose custody was all the coin which percolated through that multifarious business, and never was man prouder than when he strolled off to the strong room, with the bunch of massive, jailor-looking keys in his bony hands, as though he had the old Kandyan monarch, still safely in custody somewhere, and was going to interview him. But perhaps the most instructive sight was to see the old Clerk grapple a rebellious Moorman, or a defiant, unbelieving Chetty, refusing to take over an invoice of willow-pattern tea-pots, on account of a chip in one of the spouts, or a parcel of grey domestics, by reason of a little rustiness of the iron hoops outside the bales. Samuel would in such a delicate case inveigle the rebel into a dark Bastille-sort of room at one end of the dark inner verandah, guarded by a huge polygar dog that knew the flavour of a man's calf, and inside that gloomy sanctuary, with bolted door, such a change was wrought on the recusant buyer, as none other but the ancient clerk could have accomplished. Whether the means employed were moral, mechanical or chemical, is to this day a mystery, and whether the trade was in mamoties or muslins, Moorman or Chetty invariably came out of that ordeal, a changed man, the goods were taken over, the promissory note signed, and Samuel brought forth the baby's sheet from his cavernous pocket, and smothered his chippy visage in its ample folds in honour of the subtle victory.

In addition to all these duties Samuel was the supervisor of all the other clerks of the establishment: in the present day they would call him Director-General—he superintended their work—looked after their arithmetic and their caligraphy, and woe to the miserable man who had omitted to carry a cipher, or cross a "t" or dot an "i"! as for a blot of ink in the account sales book, we should not like to have been the guilty party, that's all. Of such rare quality was the old chief clerk's training, such cunning penmen did he turn out of hand, that many a government emissary was employed to lure Samuel to part with these precious subordinates. In vain the Treasurer made secret gorgeous offers for a trusty cashier; in vain the Auditor-General tempted him for just one single accountant. The overtures were received with scorn. Be it known that Samuel "was passing rich, on ninety pounds a-year": but then, when those ninety pounds were paid to him in rix-dollars, with figures of dropsical elephants on them, and each rix-dollar of eighteen pence British currency, would purchase half a dozen full-grown fowls or a coolie-load of eggs, or a hackery-load of country vegetables and fruit, we may form some some sort of idea of the purchasing value of the ninety pounds.

Follow him home to the paternal mansion after office hours: see him in the bosom of his family in Zuyder Street in the Pettah: what an unruffled, comfortable old Dutch bosom it was: unfortunately it spoke only in the Portuguese tongue, which in my case was a slight drawback, compelling me to converse with Samuel and his olive branches. Regularly as Christmas Day came round, the old clerk, his bosom and his branches, paid a visit to the Firm at the Colpetty mansion on which occasion there were any number of congratulations, and jokes, and questions; and after divers glasses of wine, the party went away in the happiest of moods.

On New Year's Day the visit was returned,—a goodly custom, and one which I rather think must have gone out about the time when punkahs and other modern cheap innovations came in. Clean and bright as was the chief clerk's old house in Zuyder Street, on any day in the year, it was cleaner and brighter on the New Year's festival day. The furniture was doubly bees-waxed, the walls were trebly whitewashed, and the glare of the noon-day sun was softened in that quiet abode, by drapery of the most rare and costly chintz. Even the back yard was made cool and pleasant by an umbrageous group of bananas thriving in a rich stratum of alluvial bricks chastely picked out in white. I shall not very soon forget my first New Year's visit, repeated through many seasons,—to Samuel's peaceful happy home; nor the genial glow which stole over his dry stolid features, as he held up to his bright eye, a glass of the Firm's rich creamy Cape wine, at eighteen shillings per dozen, unequalled at the figure, until he fancied he could see an embryo bee's wing in it, and how he drank the Firm's health, and the Firm drank his, and his belongings. Those were the days when Waghorn was making his great Egyptian experiment, before Reuter was invented, or cheap chemical champagne imported. A Dutch party in the Pettah, of those days, meant nine o'clock to rest, after beer and a meal of cake that would have served as capital dead-weight for any ship requiring ballast.

But changes, which belong to our common lot, overtook Colombo, and though the old clerk grown older, drew three hundred pounds per annum, he was not one whit the richer or happier. The Firm had built up a larger business, and with it had arisen a more imposing structure than the grim Dutch Office of the olden time. At Samuel's prayerful request, they had spared one portion of the old red-bricked wall, that he might feast his dim eyes on the same bricks that had been so often looked upon by his loved and honoured master, now dead and gone. He could see it from his office chair, but that large lofty room was no more the same: he found it draughty and chilly: he took cold and at last took ill, and then greatly against his will, he took a pension, but on the solemn understanding that he might attend the office once a year, to see the general accounts closed, and the balance-sheet drawn out. And this he did faithfully and cheerfully amidst growing infirmities, until at length his own earthly account was closed, by one final entry in the Wolfendahl registry.

A GALLE LEGEND.

JANZS LEYDEN was as happy and jovial as it was possible for any ordinary Custom-House clerk to be, in the sea-girt, sunny isle of Ceylon. The sleepy, apathetic peons were perfectly taken aback as they watched the ebullition of Dutch mirth that gushed from the person of the little chief clerk. The oldest Custom-House underlings did not remember to have seen so much jollity within the dark, dusky walls of that strange, straggling old building; no, not since they were little boys, and first learnt to enjoy betel. Janzs was so elated, that he made a very poor day's work of it, in his large, solitary, prison-like office: he pretended, once or twice, to be deeply immersed in some tables of exports; but it wouldn't do: one column of figures danced about before his eyes, with its *vis-a-vis*, and the totals at the bottom went up the middle and down again, to the merry country dance, which he could not leave off whistling. When he began a letter, he got to, "It having come to the knowledge of the authorities that certain kegs of brandy have"—he suddenly remembered that the man he was addressing, was hanged for smuggling last October. At last, after nibbing one or two pens, and untying and re-tying a few bundles of very neglected and extremely dusty papers with faded red-tape, he gave up the idea of being busy. The truth was, that Janzs was about to be married; that day week was to be the happy period, and as that was the first event of the kind in his life, he conceived himself privileged to be elated, and not altogether fit for office work.

Finding an excuse for closing the Custom-House at an unusually early hour, the chief clerk saw that the establishment (two subordinates, and three peons) had departed and left the old office in proper order; and then, leisurely turning the huge key in the old ironbound door, gave it to the head peon to deliver to the collector, who was, of course, quietly smoking his pipe in his own verandah. The sentry was seen to, a word exchanged with the corporal of the guard, and Janzs strutted out from under the huge dark archway which led from the strong fort of Point-de-Galle towards the suburbs, where many of the better class of burghers then resided. In those days, even the chief clerk of a public department could not afford to keep a carriage. None, indeed, but the very highest colonial officials could venture on such a piece of extravagance. This may be readily understood, when I mention that the whole of the money salary received by Janzs in one year, did not amount to more than some twenty pounds of our English currency. It is true, there were additions in the shape of fees, and allowances of oil, wood, beef, salt, and other perquisites. Nevertheless, it did not on the whole amount to more than a very decent living for a young single man.

Such being the state of affairs, it cannot be matter for surprise that Janzs should have felt certain doubts about the future rising amidst his happy dreamings, as he wended his way home to his humble low-roofed bungalow; and thence to Katrina, who dwelt with her father not far away on an old Dutch farm.

If Janzs had been happy before, how much was his delight increased when the old Dutchman, his future father-in-law, pointed out to him a fine piece of pasture-ground and woodland which he intended to give him on the wedding-day. Money he had little enough of, but he had some rich land, and the young couple were to be put in possession of some thirty acres, which might, one day, be made to yield a comfortable addition to the clerk's little income. Here was a field for Katrina and Janzs to build hopes upon. Thirty acres of forest and pasturage! The thing appeared almost too extensive to contemplate in imagination. The Fort of Galle occupied but twenty acres, and was it possible that he, a poor Custom-House clerk, should become the proprietor of half as much more land than was spanned by that sturdy, rambling, old fortress?

The next day, Janzs engaged a canoe to take them both to the identical spot; and after duty—as soon as cargoes of rice, salt-fish, and coir-rope could be hurried through the usual official routine—he hastened from the old dark office, and conducted Katrina to the bank of the river that flows from the lofty mountain peaks, past the Fort of Galle, into the Indian Ocean. Half an hour's navigation, by means of poles, took them to the scene of their speculations. They passed many a pretty retired nook, many green paddy fields and palm topes; many deep shady dells, overtopped by clustering bamboos and towering arekas, where the echo of the cool splashing waterfall was only broken by the low, soft, note of the wood-pigeon, or chattering voice of the monkey. They were delighted beyond their fondest expectations with the spot. It was so near to the town; it was so delightfully situated; it was so nicely timbered; why, there were sufficient trees upon it to build half-a-dozen bungalows, aud still leave enough for pleasant shade and firewood. And then the soil! Janzs, it is true, did not understand quite so much about agriculture, as he did of entries and bonds, and registers; but Katrina declared it was magnificent. She had never seen such soil; why, it would grow anything. In short, they both arrived at the conclusion that a handful of copper *challies*, flung broad-cast upon the ground on any showery morning, would take root before night, and grow into rix-dollars. Returning home they indulged in all sorts of wild speculations about the future. Katrina, naturally of an imaginative turn, ventured to hint at a regular farm, cows and all; and Janzs afterwards declared that she even went so far as to suggest a flock of goats; but little Katrina always denied the charge most stoutly. They were to cultivate everything that would be wanted for food or raiment, from chillies for curry up to cotton for dresses. In short, they were to have a little Eden of their own making, where discord and care should never enter; where only sweetest blossoms and flowers and richest fruits should be found; where nothing that was bad, where everything that was good, should be seen. It was to be a bright spot that "Garden by the River."

Well, they were married and were happy, as all young married people are and deserve to be, and let us hope always will be. In Ceylon, amongst the Dutch descendants to this day, it is a common occurrence for young couples to take up their abode for the first year or two of their married life under the roof of the bride or bridegroom's parents. It may be that economy sometimes renders this prudent: or it may happen that the young wife does not feel quite experienced enough to undertake housekeeping all at once, and prefers a little further schooling on many points of domestic details. Be this as it may, it was a common custom in the days I am writing of; and since Jansz was an orphan they took up their residence with old Lourenz, his new parent. The week of feasting and festivities, and congratulations over, they settled quietly down at the paternal farm, as contentedly and as happily as though it were all their own. The little stream at the bottom of the long lawn that wound round the shrubbery so coaxingly and silently, did not run more smoothly than the current of their new-found existence. Janzs toiled harder than ever at export and import duties, and occasionally expressed regret to the head store-keeper, an old white-headed Malay, that there was not double the quantity of shipping entering the port. At his new home the clerk had little to complain of. Many a sacrifice did old Lourenz make to the comfort of the young couple. Janzs had free and unlimited access to his tobacco-store and his dozen or two of venerable meerschaums. Janzs was allowed one of the oldest and most valuable drinking-horns for his own special use; and, moreover, Janzs was permitted to sit, in the cool of the evening, under the same wide-spreading mango-tree, and then, pipe in mouth, fall gently asleep, while Katrina sang an old scrap of a Dutch song, or plied her needle, or drove away the mosquitoes from her father and husband.

Yet with all this, Janzs occasionally felt not quite at ease, and was ungracious enough to vent his restless mood in presence of the father, who heeded not his desire for a little more independence, but quietly refilled his pipe, and settled the question with the unanswerable argument—pooh! pooh! Sometimes the thoughts of that sweet spot of wood and dell by the river-side came across the minds of the young people, and they sighed as they thought of the remote chance of seeing it as they had once hoped. Now and then Janzs thought of raising money upon it, to cultivate a portion at least, and erect a small bungalow; but, a stranger to such proceedings, he fancied the scheme was far too wild and visionary for a clerk upon twenty rix-dollars a month to entertain. Each time he sighed, and gave up the idea.

Katrina had observed that her father had of late been absent from the farm more frequently, and for longer intervals, than was his custom; and that, moreover, he smoked more pipes and disposed of more schiedam during the evening, under the mango-tree, than she ever remembered him to have done at any time of her life. This state of things lasted for a few months. Janzs longed more ardently than ever for emancipation; Katrina sighed for a farm of their own, and the father plied more potently at pipe and dram.

At length old Lourenz told his children that he had a mind to go and see how their little piece of land was looking, and if they would go with him, perhaps they could contrive amongst them all to plan something to be done with it. No second bidding was needed. A large covered canoe was prepared with cushions and mats, and the party started on their visit, taking with them Katrina's younger sister and brother. It was near the end of January—of all months the most agreeehble in Ceylon; the evening was so calm, and soft and fragrant; the air appeared to be as though poured down from some other and purer sphere, wafting with it songs of rich melody, and scents of rarest flowers. Nature seemed hushed and wrapped in sweetest peace. The monsters of the forests were at rest. The mountains far away flung their deep, saddening shades o'er many a league of plain: and even restless man looked forth and felt subdued.

Their light and well-manned boat went boldly up the stream, caring very little about the huge trunks of trees that at this time of year are met with in most Indian rivers, as thick as pebbles in a mill-pond. Torn from their birthplaces by inundations, they float down the rapids; until, arrested in their course by some trifling obstacle, they get embedded in the course of the river. The topes and dells and groves appeared to Katrina and her husband more beautiful than ever on that soft evening; and, had not their own loved spot been before them, they would gladly have landed a dozen times, to walk about and admire the romatic scenery. At last a bend of the river took them suddenly to where a rising wood-clad field told of their little domain.

But that could not be their land. Why, it had a beautiful little bungalow on it, and one of the sweetest gardens round it that could be imagined; all fenced and quite complete. There were outhouses, too, and a huge pile of firewood, and a nice winding path right down to the water's edge. Neither Katrina nor her husband could at first believe that they had not halted at the wrong spot: yet there was the huge Jack tree at the landing-place, and there were the yellow bamboos and the green arekas by the little stream that came tumbling down the hill-side like a child at play. Well, they both declared they had never seen such a fairy transformation: it was like a story in some Arabian book—only a great deal better; for it was all true, and would not disappear at daylight, as many of such things were said to do.

There was no end to the discoveries made by Katrina and her sister, in their rambles over the place; and though all was in a very primitive form, there was the foundation for a thousand comforts, and as many pleasures besides. Old Lourenz seated himself very quietly under a huge bread-fruit tree, and enjoyed his pipe and the contemplation of the happiness he had stealthily bestowed. Labour costs but little in the East; and most of the materials for the building had been found on the spot. Houses are seldom built of brick in Ceylon, even for government use. The best are usually made of "Cabook," a ferruginous clay easily cut from the hill-sides. It is quite soft when found; but quickly hardens on exposure to the air; and in time becomes more solid and enduring than any cement. Much of the work had been performed by the neighbouring villagers, for a little rice or tobacco; so that a great deal had been done for a very little outlay. It seemed, however, to Janzs, as though a little fortune must have been spent upon their land, and he was altogether lost in the contemplation of so much valuable property.

The following week saw them in actual possession, and Janzs taking lessons in farming from Katrina; who assured him that if he worked hard enough, and lived long enough, he would make an excellent cultivator. By small degrees, and with many kindly helps from friends and relations, the young couple found they had a tolerable establishment growing up in their charge. The clerk, at the risk of blistering his hands, toiled in the open air, morning and evening, whilst Katrina overlooked a brace of coolies, who laboured through the heat of the day. It was quite wonderful to see how things grew and prospered round and about them. No one in the district of Galle produced such delicious plantains as they grew; their poultry was allowed to be remarkably the finest in the valley; their butter the sweetest in the province, and as to bees, none thrived so well as did those of Katrina. What was better still, Janzs had, about this time, an increase to his salary of five rix dollars a month; so that, on the whole, it might, with truth, be said that they prospered; and indeed they deserved to do so, and no one thought of envying them their humble quiet happiness.

In this pleasant way a year rolled past. At that time a vessel came into the harbour, from one of the Eastern Islands, noted for its fine plantations of nutmegs; a cultivation then highly remunerative, but which the jealousy of the Dutch Government rigidly "protected," by carefully reserving it to themselves. The commander of the ship had brought with him, in a very careful manner, many hundreds of young nutmeg plants, at the request, and for the especial benefit, of the Receiver of Customs at Point de Galle. These were brought on shore in barrels of earth as ship's stores, and left in charge of Janzs; who, shortly afterwards received orders to despatch them to the country-house of his superior. One barrel was presented by the collector to the chief clerk; who, well aware of the great value of the nutmeg tree, conceived himself to be at once on the high-road to fortune.

It would be difficult to paint the satisfaction with which he knocked out the head of the barrel, on its reaching the door of his little bungalow, and feasted his own and Katrina's eyes on the sight of a hundred young nutmeg seedlings. It appeared to him as though a hundred little guardian angels had suddenly condescended to pay him a visit, to take up their abode with him for the remainder of his natural life. But what were they to do with them? Plant them, of course. Yes, but how, and where? Katrina was, for once in her little life, most completely at fault on a point of agriculture; and, it turned out on enquiry, that old Lourenz knew about as much of the proper treatment, agriculturally, of the nutmeg tree as did Janzs, or any of his office peons, or the old bald-headed Buddhist priest who lived across the river.

Great was the satisfaction of the chief clerk and his little wife to find that one of the sailors of the vessel, which had brought the plants, understood the mode of culture, and was willing to come out to their farm and put them thoroughly in the way of rearing fine nutmeg trees. Leave was obtained from the skipper, and the sailor was soon installed as hired cultivator under Katrina's own inspection. When Janzs arrived home after the first day's operations, he was astonished to find a number of moderately sized pits dug throughout his best ground, at regular and distant intervals. He was with difficulty pursuaded that these gigantic holes were necessary for the reception of the Lilliputian plants. The sailor assured him that unless the holes were made at least five feet deep, and as wide as the outer branches of the future tree were expected to extend, the plant would not thrive. The roots were of the most delicate texture; and, it was only by forming for their reception a roomy bed of light generous earth that they would be enabled to arrive at the vigour necessary for the full nourishment of the tree, and the perfection of abundant crops of fruit. Janzs held up his hands in pure astonishment; but he supposed it was all right, when the two coolies flung basket upon basket full of surface soil, and river mud, and dead leaves and weeds, into these holes; and when the sailor—gently as a nurse with a young infant, placed two seedlings in each hole, a few inches apart, filled in some more rich loamy earth around them, pressed them softly down, and then finished the ceremony by a copious baptism of river-water from a cocoanut shell—Janzs was so pleased with the imposing appearance of the new plantation that he did not heed the sailor's reason for placing the little seedlings in pairs; it was to ensure a sound, healthy plant, the stronger of the couple being left, whilst the more delicate plant was pulled out at the end of the first six months.

This, however, was not all the care that was needed for the young plants. A score of contingencies had to be guarded against. There might be too much sun, or too much wet, or the wind might loosen them and injure the roots. Cattle or wild animals might get at them, and browse on their tender leaves, which would be fatal to them, Insects might prey upon the young shoot or the new bark. So that although, as Katrina was assured, when the trees did survive all these dangers, they would be certain to yield a lasting and golden harvest, it would not be without a long trial of watchfulness and care. But she was not easily daunted; the prospect of the future cheered on her little heart against all misgivings. She made the sailor-planter show her how they fenced in the nutmeg trees at Penang and the Moluccas: how they sheltered them from the scorching rays of the noonday sun, and how they protected them from the nocturnal attacks of porcupines and wild hogs, by weaving prickly boughs around them on the ground. Katrina felt quite sure that she could manage the whole plantation, and bring every tree to full bearing; and the sailor took his leave, loaded with thanks and homely gifts. Janzs thought himself the luckiest and happiest of Custom-House clerks, to possess such a wife, and such a garden of nutmeg trees.

Years rolled on in Ceylon, much as such portions of time are in the habit of doing in other places. They brought with them changes in men and things at the little sturdy fort of Galle, not less than elsewhere. Few changes, perhaps, were more apparent than those which were perceptible in the nutmeg plantation I have described. The little white-washed bungalow had spread forth wings on either side, and front and ends were shadowed by jessamines and roses. Topes of waving cocoa, and sago palms, and broad-leaved bananas flung a grateful shade over the lawn, and the sweet flower garden, and the path to the river-side. The Lilliputian seedlings were no longer there, but in their places rose, proudly and gracefully, a whole forest of bright-leaved, flower-spangled nutmeg trees: and amongst them might be seen, if you looked in the right place, Katrina, still busy, and smiling, and happy with Janzs by her side, and a group of little rollicking children revelling on the soft green grass. Unwearying care and watchfulness had wrought wonders with those delicate nutmegs; and now the time had arrived when they were about to reap the rich reward of perseverance and industry. Janzs considered himself, as well he might, a man of some substance. In a year or two, or more, all those beautiful trees would be in full bearing; and if, as they gave promise to do, they bore two or three hundred nuts each, there would be a little fortune for him; a larger yearly revenue than was enjoyed by his superior, the Collector of Customs, and all the clerks and peons together.

Fate, however, had decreed that all this was not to be. Those richly promising trees were doomed to an early and sudden death.

I mentioned how the collector had obtained a vast quantity of these young nutmeg plants. There were several thousands of them, and their cultivation had cost him some money, and more trouble. But whether it was that he selected bad land, or had them planted improperly, or neglected them afterwards, there is nothing on record to tell. Certain it is, that his large plantation became a complete failure, much to his vexation. This was no whit lessened, when he learnt, and afterwards witnessed, the entire success of his subordinate Janzs with his little garden of nutmeg trees.

VanDort, the collector, was a small-minded, mean-spirited creature, as you will soon see. He brooded over his disappointment for many a long day; until at length, in the very abjectness of his low heart, he thought that if he could not succeed, neither should Janzs. He knew right well that there was an old order in council, forbidding any one in the States-General's possessions in the East Indies, to cultivate spices, save and except in such islands as they declared to be so privileged; namely, Ceylon for cinnamon and pepper, and Moluccas and

Penang for the nutmeg and cloves. Confiscation and imprisonment for the first offence were the mild consequences of infringing this law. What the second offence was to be visited with, was not exactly known ; but better lawyers than Janzs, were haunted with an indistinct vision, that in such a case was made and provided nothing short of the gallows. Now, Mynheer Van Dort was well aware of the existence of this severe order when he planted his large piece of ground; but he had reckoned on being able to sell his plantation and retire to Europe before the authorities at Colombo could hear anything of the matter; for, in all probability, there were not three persons in the island who knew of the existence of such stringent laws. It occurred to him that, as he had failed and nearly all his trees had died, he might turn the success of his clerk to good account on his own behalf, by informing the Governor of the bold infraction of the laws by Janzs.

In those quiet, by-gone times, there were but few events of importance to call for any exercise of power by the highest authority in the colony. It was therefore, with no little bustle that the Governor summoned his council to consider and determine upon the contents of a weighty despatch received from Point de Galle. This was the letter of VanDort the collector, informing them of the high criminality of his subordinate. It did not require much deliberation to settle the course to be pursued. The forbidden trees were ordered to be forthwith cut down, the property confiscated, Janzs to be imprisoned for five years, and the zealous collector to be rewarded with promotion on the first opportunity.

Turn once more to the quiet, bright spot, the garden by the river. Janzs was home as usual from his daily duties. It was evening. Katrina had given her last orders to the gardener and the stock-keeper. The children were gambolling on the green-sward under the large mango-tree. The favourite nutmeg trees were heavy with blossom; the sun was still lingering amongst the topmost branches of the jambo trees. Everything gave promise of one more of those many happy evenings so prized and loved by Janzs and his little wife, when a canoe dashed heavily against the river-bank, and forth from it sprang the fiscal of the district, attended closely by a half-dozen of sturdy, grim looking Malay peons, armed with swords and pikes. The officer of the Crown knew Janzs well; and, though inclined to be friendly towards him, had no alternative but to tell him, in a few words, the purport of his visit, and the cause—those bright-leaved trees waving to the breeze, and alive with merry blossoms. The poor clerk could be with difficulty persuaded of the reality of the sad news. A sight of the Governor's warrant, however, settled all doubts, and Janzs shortly afterwards staggered to the boat, between two peons, like a drunken man. Katrina saw him to the water's edge, and bade him be of good cheer, for all would yet be well; though her sinking heart gave the lie to her lips.

The work of destruction did not occupy much time. Four peons, with sharp axes, made but a small matter of those young and delicate trees; and, in about half the time that was usually spent in watering them, they were all laid prostrate on the ground. The clicking of those bright axes fell sadly enough on Katrina's ear; each blow seemed to her to be a deadly wound aimed at herself, and as the last of those long-tended and much-loved trees fell heavily to the ground, her courage and spirits fled, and she gave vent to her feelings in a flood of tears.

Next morning she left that once loved spot, sad and spiritless; and, taking her little ones with her, placed them in safety with her father. She then sought her husband in his prison, to comfort and console him, as best she might. None there knew whence the blow came: so little, indeed, did the sufferers dream of how matters stood, that, a few days after the catastrophe, Katrina waited on the collector, and besought him, for the sake of Janzs' long service, to intercede for him, and obtain a remission of the cruel sentence.

Weeks passed away, and it appeared that there was small chance of any pardon from the Governor, who viewed with the greatest displeasure any contravention of the Imperial laws. Janzs abandoned himself to despair: his friends considered him a lost man. All but Katrina gave up hoping for him. She never for a moment lost sight of any chance which seemed to promise success. Night and day she sought for some friendly aid to carry out her plan. That scheme was to present a petition to the Governor, in person: he was reported to be a just man, though despotic in the administration of the laws. Katrina felt certain that he knew not all the facts of their little history, though the collector had assured her everything had been told him. Amongst others whom she sought for advice and aid, was the minister of their little church, who listened to her with the patience of a child. He knew a good deal of their history, though not aware of the facts connected with their possession of the fatal nutmegs. He heard Katrina tell her sad story, pitied her, condoled with her, bade her to be of good cheer, and finally sent her away, full of faith and hope.

The good old minister saw at once the wickedness of the collector, for he knew who had laid the charge against Janzs. He went boldly, though carefully, to work: satisfied himself of the fact of Van Dort having planted nutmegs on a larger scale than his clerk, though unsuccessfully: drew up a petition to the Governor, obtained the signature of Janzs, and then proceeded with it to Colombo, and laid it with his own hands at the feet of their ruler. The good man was heard patiently, and in twenty-four hours after perusal of the petition, instructions were sent off to Galle to the Commandant, to institute the most searching inquiry into the whole case.

It only remains to relate how the wicked collector was detected, and dismissed the service. Janzs was not only restored to the possession of his lands, but received the appointment of collector of Galle, as compensation for his imprisonment. And so all went well. None was more delighted than Katrina, who, however, would not be satisfied until they were once more quietly settled on their pretty farm, by the river side. There, for long years afterwards, they lived in the enjoyment of health and ample means, which were, after all, brought them, indirectly, by their nutmeg plantation: and though none of those ominous trees were any longer growing, there were hundreds of others, which yielded ample stores of luscious grateful fruit, and flung a cool and balmy shade o'er streams and flowers, in many a quiet nook of that sweet garden by the river.

A PEEP AT THE "PERAHERRA."

OF the religious festivals of the Buddhists of Ceylon, that known as the Peraherra is the most important. It is observed at Kandy, the capital of the ancient Kings of Ceylon, and at Ratnapoora the chief town of the Saffragam district. Few good Buddhists will be absent from these religious observances; and whole families may be seen journeying on foot for many miles, over mountains, through dense jungles and unwholesome swamps, along hot, sandy pathways, loaded with their pittance of food and the more bulky presents of fruit, rice, oil, and flowers, to lay upon the holy shrine of Buddha, to be eventually devoured by the insatiable priests.

In the month of July, 1840, I had a peep at the celebrated Peraherra of Ratnapoora, where the shrine sacred to the memory of Saman, rivals in attraction the great Dalada Maligawa of Kandy. Like its mountain competitor, it has its relic of Buddha enshrined in a richly jewelled casket, which is made an object of especial veneration to the votaries of that god. Saman was the brother of the famed Rama, the Malabar conqueror who invaded Ceylon in ages long past, and extirpated from its flowery shores the race of mighty giants who had held its people in subjection for many centuries, a sort of oriental King Arthur. To Saman was given the district of Saffragam; and the people of that country at his death, promoted him to the dignity of a deity, as a slight token of their regard.

The Ratnapoora festival is the more attractive by reason of its being made the occasion of a large traffic in precious stones, with which the neighbourhood abounds. In this way the great part of the Buddhists manage to combine commerce with devotion.

The road to the Saffragam district was, in the time at which I travelled along it, a very barbarous and dangerous affair, differing widely from the excellent traces which existed through most of the maritime provinces of Ceylon. It was then, in fact, little more than a mere bullock-track, or bridle-path, with no bridges to aid in crossing the streams which intersect it. The journey from Colombo to Ratnapoora may now be easily performed in one day: at that time it required a good nag and careful diligence to accomplish it in two; whilst swollen rivers often caused serious delay.

Day dawned as I got clear of the Pettah or Black Town of Colombo, and crossed a small stream which led me to the jungle or village road I was to follow. In England, we should call such a muddy lane; but here one knows little between the good high roads and the bullock-track. Strange as it may sound to home travellers, one is often glad to see the sun rise, and feel it warm the heavy, damp air in the tropics. Before me lay a long straggling line of low jungle, indicating the road: far away in the distance rose the high, bluff hill and rocks towering over the once royal domain of Avishawella. Around on every side, was water, completely hiding the fields from view and only allowing a bush or a tree, or a hut-top, to be seen peeping up through the aqueous veil, dotting the wide expanse like daisies in a field. The rains had flooded the whole of the low country which, inundated by many mountain torrents, could not discharge the mass of streams nearly so fast as it received them. Over and across all this watery wilderness huge masses of misty vapour came rolling and tumbling along as though shrouding some titanic water-sprites who had been keeping it up rather late the night before, and were not quite sure of the way home. One might have imagined indeed, that it was some universal washing-day and that the great lid of the national copper had just been lifted.

As the sun rose above the line of black rocks in the distance, its rays lit up those misty monsters of the flood, imparting to them life-like tints, which gave them beauty, and forms they had not known before. As these sun-lit fogs rolled on, a thousand shapes moved fitfully amongst them; troops of wild horsemen; crystal places with gilded gates; grim figures playing at bo-peep; hills, towns, and castles; with many a ship at sea, and lovely cottages in quiet sunny glades;—all these, and more seemed there. With the sea breeze, all that array of cloudy creations departed, leaving the air hot and stifling from the reflection of the sun's rays in the endless flood about me. But where were the poor Singalese villagers, their families, and their goods, amidst all this wreck? As I jogged along, the cry of a child, the crowing of a cock the bark of a dog floated across the ocean of mist, but whence came they? I looked to the right and to the left. I strained my eyes straightforward, but not a soul, or a feather, or a head was to be seen. Presently the fog cleared away, and I could see over-head into the trees. There chairs, tables, chatties paddy-pounders, boxes of cloths, children in cots, men, women, cats, dogs, all were seen in one strange medley, curiously ensconsed amongst the wide-spreading branches of the trees. Over their heads and on each side, mats and cocoanut leaves were hung to keep off rain and damp fogs, whilst against each side of the tree was placed a thick notched stick, which served as a ladder for the whole party. Here and there canoes were to be seen paddled across the fields, to keep up communication between the different villages. It was a strange but desolate spectacle, and I was glad to find myself, at last, free from the watery neighbourhood, and once more riding on terra firma,

During the heat of the next day I turned aside to a shady green lane. A mile along this quiet pathway I was tempted to rest myself at the mouth of a dark-looking cave, by the side of a running stream of mountain water. Tying my pony to a bush I entered at the low archway, and found myself at once in utter darkness; but after a short time I began to distinguish objects, and then saw, close to me, one whom I should have least looked for in that strange, desolate spot. It was a Chinaman, tail and all. My first idea was as I looked at the figure through the dim light of the cave, that it was nothing more than a large China jar, or, perhaps a huge tea-chest, left there by some traveller; but when the great, round face relaxed into a grin, and the little pea-like eyes winked, and the tail moved, and the thick lips uttered broken English, I took a proper view of the matter, and wished my cavern acquaintance "good morning." I soon gathered the occupation of Lee-Chee in this strange place; the cave we were then in, was one of the many in that neighbourhood, in which a particular kind of swallow builds the edible nests so highly prized by the Chinese and Japanese for conversion into soups, stews, and for ought we know, into tarts. The Chinaman told me what I was scarcely prepared to learn, that he rented from the Ceylon Government the privilege to seek these birds' nests in the district, for which he paid the yearly sum of one hundred dollars, or seven pounds, ten shillings. Procuring a chule, or native torch, the Chinese nest hunter showed me long ledges of shelving rock at the top of the cavern whereon whole legions of curious little gummy-like excrescences were suspended; some were perfect nests, others were in course of formation, and these latter I learnt were the most valued; those which had had the young birds reared in them being indifferently thought of, and were only bought by the lower orders of soup makers. Having rested myself and pony I once more pushed on for Ratnapoora, where I arrived, heated, jaded, and dusty, by high noon.

A chattie bath seldom fails to refresh the Indian traveller, and fit him for the enjoyment of his meal. In the cool of the evening I strolled out to watch the preparations for the nightly festivities. These continue for about a fortnight, chiefly after sunset, though devotees may be seen laying their simple offerings at the foot of the shrine, during most part of the afternoon. The little bazaar of the town was alive with business; all vestiges of its wonted filth and wretchedness were hidden beneath long strips of white linen and garlands of cocoanut leaves and flowers hung around by bands of bright red cloth. Piles of tempting wares were there; beads, bangles, and scarfs to decorate; rice, jaggery, and sweetmeats to eat, and innumerable liquors to drink, were placed in profuse array. The streets and lanes poured forth long strings of human beings, heated with the sun, flushed with drink, and bedizened with trumpery jewellery, and mock finery. Poor tillers of the soil; beggarly fishermen; mendicant peelers; half-starved coolies; lean, sickly women, and poor, immature children, passed onwards in the motley throng, burying their every-day misery beneath the wild mirth of a night or two at the Peraherra.

Following the living dark stream, as closely as the heat, dust and strange odours would allow me, I arrived, at length, near to the Temple of Saman. The edifice, of which I caught a distant glimpse, was half concealed beneath the heavy luxuriant foliage of cocoanut topes, arekas, plantains, and banyan trees. An ocean of human heads filled up the space around the building, from which proceeded the well-known sounds of the reed and tom-tom. Gay flags fluttered from the four corners and the lofty pinnacle in the centre; wreaths of flowers, plaited leaves and ribbons of many colours waved jauntily from roof to door; whilst round the pillars of the walls and door-posts clustered rich bunches of most tempting fruit.

Close by this busy scene, another group was forming under a large and lofty pandahl, or open bungalow. Forcing my way to one corner of the shed, I found a company of Indian jugglers consisting of two men, a girl and a child of perhaps three years. The men were habited in strange uncouth dresses, with large strings of heavy black beads round their necks; the girl was simply and neatly clad in white with silver bangles and anklets, and a necklace of native diamonds. It would be impossible to detail all their extraordinary performances, which far exceeded anything I had ever read of their art. The quantity of iron and brass-ware which they contrived to swallow was truly marvellous; ten penny nails, clasp-knives, &c., were all treated as so many items of pastry on confectionary, and I could but picture to myself the havoc a dozen of these cormorants would commit in an ironmonger's shop.

Near the temple all was noise and confusion, and it was with some difficulty that I forced my way through the dense crowd, and reached the steps of the venerated shrine. The priest stationed at the entrance made a way in for me as well as he could, but the pressure inside was intense. Hundreds of men and women pressed eagerly forward to reach the flight of steep stone stairs which led up to the sacred depositary. It was as bad as a crush to get into the Crystal Palace. My passage was so slow that I had time to examine and admire the fine antique carved work on the pillars and ceiling of the entrance-hall, as well as on the tall pilasters which lined the ample staircase. There was a beauty of style and a high degree of finish about this work that could not be attained in Ceylon in the present day. Arrived, at length, at the inner temple or sacred shrine above, I passed with the rest, between a richly brocaded curtain which hung in folds across the entrance at the top of the stairs, and stood before the famed relic of Buddha or rather the jewelled casket which contained it. I felt disappointment at the spectacle here, arising, perhaps from my taking no interest in the exhibition as a religious ceremony, and looking at it merely as an empty show, not far removed from the status of Bartholomew Fair. The strong glare of a hundred lights, the heat and crowd of so many in so small a place, the sickly perfume of the piles of

Buddha flowers heaped before the shrine by the pilgrims, the deafening discordant din of a score of tom-toms and vile screeching pipes, made me glad enough to descend the stairs and flinging a rupee into the poor-box of the temple, to escape once more into fresh air.

From the votaries of Saman I entered another crowd, assembled round a gaily decorated building, which I at once perceived was a Hindoo temple. Here to the sound of much music, and by the light of many lamps a group of young dancing girls were delighting the motley crowd. There were but three of them, one a finely-made, tall, sylph-like creature with really graceful movements; the others younger, stouter and far less pleasing. A good deal of pains had evidently been taken with their dress, to the value of twenty thousand dollars. The graceful little jacket which the chief dancer wore over her flowing white robes, sparkled and glistened with something which was quite new to me as articles of ornament: along the edge of her pure white garment shone a whole host of fire-flies which by some ingenious arrangement had been secured to the dress, and gave a strange and pleasing novelty to the appearance of her attire, as she swept gracefully around in slow and measured steps. The music to which these people dance is anything but pleasing to an English ear: indeed, there is scarcely a trace of rhythm in it; yet they contrive to measure their mazy and difficult dance by its notes with admirable precision. Long custom has so attached them to their empty meaningless music that they can appreciate no other. I am certain that M. Julien's band would scarcely be listened to by the Singalese if there were a few tom-toms within hearing. It is a curious fact that in the districts from which these Nautch girls are brought, education is so rare that they are generally the only lay persons within many days' journey, who can either read or write. The priests can all read, if not write, and they take care to instruct the temple girls in order to enable them to learn the various songs and legends for recital at their periodic festivals. The rest of the population they keep in the densest ignorance.

Leaving the dancers and priests I strolled towards the broad Kaloo-ganga, whose quiet, palm-shaded banks stood out in the sweetest contrast to the noisy revelry I had just beheld. The moon was near the full, and rising high above the many rich green topes of palms and drooping plantains, lit up the peaceful scene with marvellous radiance. It is hardly possible to conceive the magic beauty of moonlight in the tropics: those who have witnessed it can never forget their feeling under its influence. The master hand of our finest painters might attempt to depict it, but the affair would be a dead failure; and did it succeed, strangers to these climes would pronounce it an unnatural painting. Even in its reality it bears the impress of something half unearthy, and it requires the testimony of the huge feathery leaves as they wave to the breeze, to assure one that the whole scene is not fictitious. Fully as bright and radiating, though softer in its hue than the broad sunshine, the moon poured down in living streams its gifts of ether-light. The monster palms, the slender arekas, the feathery bamboos and tamarinds revelled in the harmony and glow of radiant moonlight, which, leaping down in phosphorescent waves sprang on from leaf to flower, from bud to herb, and streaming through the waving seas of giant, emerald grass, died sparkling at its feet.

Some of the topes along this gentle river grew so thickly that not the faintest ray of light found its soft way amongst them: the deepest shade was there, and only in one of these could I trace any vestiges of living beings. A little hut was buried far away in the inmost recesses of a tope, all bright above, all gloom below. The door was open, and from it shone a faintly glimmering light; so tiny was the ray amidst that heavy shade, so distant did it seem, that it defied all conception of space, and made my eyes ache to gaze at it. I, at length, distinguished faint sounds proceeding from it. They were those of a regular harmony. Strolling nearer I heard that they proceeded from cultivated voices. What a sensation! The music was that of the "Evening Hymn!" and it came upon me with the echoes of the uncouth Babel of heathenism I had just left, still ringing in my ears. When I recovered from the pleasant surprise, I found that the singers were the family of a native missionary who had embraced Christianity.

The next day the bazaar was crowded with dealers in and diggers for precious stones. Hundreds of Moormen, Chetties, Arabs, Parsees, and Singalese were busily employed in the barter; and a most noisy operation it was. In the neighbourhood of Ratnapoora exist many tracts of clayey and gravelly land, rich in rubies, sapphires, garnets, turquoise, and cats-eyes. For the privilege of digging for these or of sifting them from the sands of some of the rivers, the natives pay heavy rents to Government; often sub-letting the ground, at large profits, to needy speculators. Their harvest is usually offered for sale during the Peraherra; and be their gains what they may they are generally rid of the whole amount before the end of the festival. The existence of this source of wealth is unfortunately, a bane rather than a blessing to the district; for whole villages flock to the gem-grounds, delving and sifting for weeks together, utterly neglecting their rice fields and gardens. Arrack taverns have multiplied, intemperance has increased, long tracts of fertile land have ceased to be sown with paddy, and the country people often buy their food from strangers in place of growing it, as formerly.

Struggling and forcing a way through the busy crowd were to be seen one or two Hindoo fakeers, most repulsive objects, depending for subsistence on the alms of pilgrims and others. One of these wretched creatures, in the fulfilment of a vow, or as an act of fancied righteousness, had held his left arm for so many years erect above his head, that it could not now be moved—and grew transfixed, emaciated and bony. It seemed more like a dry, withered stick tied to the body, than a part of itself. The other fakeer had closed his hands for so long a period that the finger-nails had grown through the palms and projected at the back of them: these miserable-looking objects appeared to reap a tolerable harvest, and seemed to be then in no pain.

Under the shade of a banyan tree, a grave-looking Moorman was amusing a crowd of boys and women with the recital of some wonderful legend or silly tale. The trade of story-telling, in the East, is still a profitable one, if I might judge from the comfortable appearance of this well-clad talker.

When I left Ratnapoora crowds were still flocking into the town, for on the morrow the huge temple elephants were expected to march in procession through the place, decked out in all kinds of finery, but it was a wearisome spectacle, and I was heartily glad to find myself once more on my pony quietly winding through green paddy-fields and under shady topes.

OLD ENGLISH COLOMBO.

OLD Colombo,—the Colombo of our early days,—the heart of our city,—the Colombo "Fort" of the good, old sleepy times, is numbered with the things which form a part of history. The pick and mamotie have undone the solid work of many weary years. What once formed the glory of that rare, old, sturdy fortress, is levelled to the dust and trampled under foot. Coolies with alavangahs have effected what no enemy ever dared attempt, for it was found, when cannon were brought to bear experimentally on the walls at short range, the heavy round shot had no effect but to find a resting-place within the earthen bowels that lay beyond the massive walls.

The picturesque in these modern days cannot hold its own against the practical—effect must yield to usefulness, and so the grass-grown battlements, the fine old crooked soorya trees, the bastions, the loop holed walls, the ancient gateway, the heavy drawbridge, fell to make Colombo more spacious, breezy and healthful, but not more cheerful to look on. We miss the rare old walls and their many associations, although changes have come over the place since first it was Colombo, and even in this our own time we fail to recognise some portions that we knew of old. All that remain of the ancient fort and its dwellings are here and there a few old Dutch houses, ancient gable-ends that had never seen aught but one or two straggling passers-by, and the few sooriya trees and mouldy walls over the way: these may now look out across an open space upon old ocean, and watch the white-sailed merchantman float to the horizon like some bright nautilus until it fades from sight.

The labyrinthine entrance to the fort, scarce wide enough for two carriages to pass, gave the old grim moat and gateway a smack of feudal times, savoring of old mystery, and of beleaguering armies which made war against those sturdy battlements, but all in vain.

And the dear old shady walks upon the ramparts, whence we have for many a year looked out upon the setting sun, and watched the tiny sails of fishing craft melting away in distance, until lost amidst fleecy clouds on the horizon.

To the resident of the present time the Pettah is sought as rarely as possible; the heat and noisy crowd and choking dust, giving it an unenviable reputation. Who would linger there from choice: who passes through it but from necessity. But let us invoke the aid of some good spirit and conjure up an evening scene in that same quarter forty years ago.

At the sea-side corner of Main Street looking out upon the Racket Court ground and the Lotus Pond, stand one or two quaint old tenements. In one of these was born and passed his infancy, the late Queen's Advocate, a man who left his mark behind him. At the opposite corner, overlooking the burial-ground is a long stretch of buildings with upper floors and verandahs skirting the side street and large Dutch rooms with ample doors and windows. Here dwells a thrifty, busy, carriage-builder and harness-maker destined at a later date to lay the foundation of an ample fortune by means of Coffee planting, then in its infancy: beyond these on either side, shaded by pretty sooriya and a few oleander trees, the wide verandahs are alive with Burghers and their numerous little ones. Each dwelling has its quota: lamps are burning brightly above them, the sound of merry laughter in all, of songs and music in many, make up a living panorama that the traveller through the Pettah of to-day could not realise. Beyond these dusty limits, and away down Sea Street there has been no change within the memory of living man. The same crowded fraternity of gauze-clad, portly Chetties, with cold calculating eyes and thirfty ways, lodged in the same human warrens with the same gaily-colored ships painted on the house walls, floating on seas of rainbow hues. The Hindoo temple is perhaps somewhat more wickedly ornate and horribly grotesque than of old, but otherwise there is no change in the thronged Chetties' quarters. From early morning till far into the hours of night these eager thrifty dealers, toil ever, fattening on their ceaseless industry.

Kayman's Gate, a gate no longer, where a Swiss Guard once kept watch and ward, is still the busy centre of a poor and struggling population. The half-fed mechanic may be seen following his vocation at all hours. The old Tinker at the corner who combines the art of soldering leaky coffee pots and ramshackled lanthorns, with the more important craft of undertaker, slaves at his task all through the sultry day, chatting at odd moments with the small children, who by means of coir-yarn bridles are playing at horses on a pile of coffins close-by.

From these scenes outside the walls let us in imagination pass across the drawbridge, and entering the crooked gateway, take a survey of the streets within the Fort, when the evening meal is over, and the residents, civil, military, and mercantile, are lounging in their verandahs, or dropping in upon neighbours, which in those primitive times, was the custom. The streets are still where they were, but how changed the dwellings and the dwellers! One by one the old tenements have given place to lofty offices, and now how few old buildings remain to tell the story of other times.

In those days there were not many European residents outside the fort. A straggling few in the near portion of Colpetty: one or two in Slave Island and at Kew-point, and Captain's Garden; and about as many in Mutwall. The majority by far dwelt within the walls. High military officials resided in those times within walls which form to-day a tailor's cutting room in Hospital lane. Merchants resided in one half of a house, whilst they carried on their business in the other portion; and when the day's work was over, the verandah in front formed the family sitting-room, to which military and civilian neighbours resorted as a matter of course. Queen Street looked in upon Prince Street, whilst hospitalities were exchanged between Baillie Street, and Chatham Street. A stroll through the fort after dinner was a pleasant mode of passing the time, dropping in first on one neighbour and then on another, until the evening round was completed. The sound of music and of mirth resounded within the old grim, grass-grown walls; and if in those days society were small and amusements few and simple, there were rarely complaints of dulness: early hours were the rule, though there were a few roystering mercantile or military spirits, men of a stamp that have long since passed away, who too often for their healths' sake, held revels towards the hours of morning. Tradition has told how once when some of these roysterers were trenching upon daylight and during a heavy pause between their songs and laughter, the voices of birds just waking, thrilled in their ears from the branches of a Sooriya tree close by. Enraged at the tiny voiced rebuke, one of the revellers called to a sleepy servant, "Boy, go out, and stop the noise of those confounded birds!"

Young officers then dwelt in Baillie Street; and well do I remember the astonishment caused by the discovery of a huge coach-wheel beneath the wooden flooring of one of the humble tenements on the occasion of some repairs being carried on, and how the neighbours were puzzled to account for its deposit there, until old De Silva, the ancient clerk of the Kandy coach office, hearing of the discovery, recognised the wheel and remembered its history. Two young officers of H.M. 18th Irish, lived once upon a time in that identical house, and Silva remembered well when the coach office was just opposite, and how early one morning when the coach was about to be horsed in its tri-weekly journey to Kandy, one of the wheels was missing. Search was made in vain: the wheel was never discovered, and the consequence was that no coach left that day for the mountain capital. The young officers had hidden the wheel under the wooden flooring of their bedroom, and there it had remained until accidently unearthed.

In these latter times coffee has changed all this. Merchants need every foot of room that is available within the Fort. Officers have been driven to their military quarters: Civilians have taken flight in all directions; and now, without the walls, rice is doing in the Pettah, what coffee has accomplished within. The Burgher element has receded before the absorbing Chetties and Moormen, and one may stroll along Main Street or Keyzer Street on any fine moonlight night, and hear no sound of music, or soft voice within the walls, meet no graceful forms, and see no dark bright eye, or well turned ancle in wide, illuminated verandahs.

"OLD JOE."

IN the early days of commercial life in the East, when the pagoda tree flourished in Ceylon ready to be shaken by any resolute hand, "Old Joe" reigned supreme in Colombo Bachelors' society, as the King of Good Fellows—the Lord of conviviality. The smallness of the unofficial circle in those primitive times, was fully compensated for by the extent of its hospitality. No strangers of any respectability, no commanders of any of the few ships which frequented our port, were allowed to take refuge in the dreary wastes of the Government Rest House—a sombre, low-roofed building, which occupied the site of the present Telegraph Offices. There was a hearty welcome; a cordial greeting, under the roof of each one of the mercantile community, with detached rooms in the rear of their houses for bachelors, and hot tiffin at the offices in the fort, that could at any time be made to do duty for a hearty dinner.

The subject of this notice was the head, and, I might add, the body of a commercial firm of good position: the other partner consituted the legs, running about in all possible directions, touting for business, and, it was whispered, not particular as to how he obtained it. "Joe" was the impersonation of honor: Donald was supposed to have been, if not the inventor, at any rate, the most diligent propounder of the philosophic maxim, "Make money, honestly if you can, but make money." So completely were they the representatives of opposites, that no one would have believed they could have continued long together as partners in business: nor would they but that each was content to let the other "gang his ain gait." Had Donald's name been Phelim or Rory, you would still have felt persuaded he was from north of the Tweed: whilst on the other hand nobody could undertake to affirm, and indeed, nobody cared whether Joe had been born north or south of the border-country.

In business matters Donald was the touter, Joe was the purveyor. What one angled for and landed, the other preserved, and usually, with consummate good humour and unbroken faith. How often was the senior hurt and vexed by the promises of his junior, so difficult of realisation: how coarsely savage was the other with the scrupulous exactitude with which every business stipulation was more than fulfilled in the spirit, if not in the letter. Donald was the ogre, the evil genius of the office: from dewy morn to sultry eve his chief aim appeared to be to make every wretched subordinate still more wretched than he was, by fault-finding, by fining, by storming; in fact, by every conceivable mode of worrying. It was joyous and thrilling to hear the sound "ship-in-sight," from the flag-staff orderly, as he peeped into the ogre's den; for all knew they would be free from their tormentor for that day, and perhaps, the following. Thrusting the huge, broad-brimmed, whitey-brown fluffy beaver on his uncombed, shaggy head; snatching up his ponderous white cotton umbrella, and grasping in one hand a long tin case of estate plans, he made rapidly for the wharf, and slipping into the first canoe, ordered the boatman to pull off to the strange ship, the first to board her in the hope of catching a constituent or two in want of a fine block of land in an accessible, salubrious and picturesque district, of which his firm always had a number on hand, ready surveyed, with the boundaries and bridle-paths cut.

The whole establishment, from the Dutch book-keeper down to the Tamil office sweeper and errand boy, breathed more freely; and nothing in this sublunary sphere would have caused them collectively and individually more heartfelt satisfaction than for a gale of wind to have sprung up and carried a particular canoe round the Island as far as the Great Basses, or, for the matter of that, to Trincomalie.

The book-keeper strolled into the cool, inner office, where was seated old Joe in loose attire, his shirt front flung wide open, with two or three letters upon his desk waiting replies at a convenient season. The burly chief treated his head clerk as a trusted, faithful servant, and did not scruple to consult him on many a knotty point in native dealings or European commerce. The office-boy, no longer awed by Donald's presence, peeped in at the sanctum door, revelled for a few moments in the refulgence of the great presence within, and then stepped to the back verandah, where he listened to stories from the one-eyed bottle-washer who was preparing for racking off three whole casks of Hodgson and Abbot's pale ale.

Four o'clock was the signal for closing up the heavy work of the day, and preparing for the outgoing tappal; for at that date, there was but a mail coach to Kandy on each alternate day, and none other. At the half hour, neighbours looked in; York Street came round the corner, King Street looked up the Chief of Prince Street, and there being no Chamber of Commerce, old Joe's was the established house of call for most of the mercantile community without families to take them home. But how compact that body: seven firms, three of them with married partners, left about half a dozen commercial bachelors as the declared votaries of the rosy god.

The daily, or rather nightly round of social life in those Colombo days, must, if the historian keep a faithful record, be pronounced decidedly fast, and occasionally furious, carried too often into the wee hours of the morning. At old Joe's the nocturnal arrangements were discussed and determined: sometimes the party were to meet at the chief bachelor's mansion, closely adjoining Captain's Garden; sometimes in the long back office room at the fort premises of Blackbird and Company, one of the few old Dutch houses still remaining in Prince Street, facing the General Post Office: but regularly once a week from Saturday noon until early on Monday morning, the resort of these jovial worshippers of Bacchus was the old Whist

Bungalow, so named from the card parties made up there on the Saturday night (we will say nothing about Sunday) when they were joined by Jock Anderson and some few other kindred spirits of the Ceylon Rifle Regiment. To attempt a sketch of the scenes enacted within that river-side bungalow, famed later for its many happy family gatherings, is beyond my power and present purpose. Suffice it to say, that one Saturday night was spent pretty much as another, varied only by the guests who drove down to Mutwall point to partake of the fun and frolic.

On some occasions cards were ignored: when, an unusually large number of the "Rifles" were present, more especially, when Jock and a well-remembered theatrical member of the Bar were there, the festive board had attractions superior to the whist table, and songs, nay, even dances, formed the staple of the nocturnal revels. I may here mention the fact that "Old Joe" though burly in person, was nimble of foot, and a most graceful dancer, despite his bulk. Many a time and oft, towards the small hours of the morning, the ponderous old Dutch table at whist bungalow would be cleared of all bottles and glass, and "Joe" being called upon, kicking off his shoes would dance one of his favorite Highland dances, a reel, or fling whatever it might chance to be, on the well polished surface.

At this same bungalow there were on Sundays, meetings of what were known as the Beef Steak Club, the members of which composed of merchants, military officers, and civil servants, met there to discuss the best beef-steaks that could be procured, and the ripest of country-bottled ale from the only recognised brewery of those days—Hodgson and Abbot's. It was in connection with one of these Sunday afternoon parties, elongated well into evening hours, that a characteristic story is related of Jock Anderson. Brave as a lion, the major was docile as a lamb towards the juniors of his regiment, whom he appeared to regard as his special protégés. One of the senior lieutenants but recently arrived from Europe, had a turn for bullying, and on one occasion went so far with his insolence towards one of the young subs present, that it became evident the new comer was bent on a quarrel. Seeing this, Jock Anderson rose and tapping the irrepressible lieutenant on the shoulder, beckoned him to follow into the verandah. There, in a few blunt words, the major gave the other a piece of his mind. "They were there as the guests of the merchants, and the harmony of the evening must not and should not be disturbed. It was evident lieutenant so-and so wished to provoke a duel, but he, the major never allowed "his boys" to go out, he always acted for them, and on the present occasion, by—dash—he would be found ready the next morning at gun-fire to put a bullet through any part of the lieutenant's body he choose to name,—and by—dash—he'd do it too."—It is scarcely necessary to add that the major's reputation as a shot was such that the quarrelsome party subsided, and slunk back to the table, a subdued and peaceful man.

PHILLIP OF BRASSFOUNDER STREET.

IN eastern countries as well as in the west, there is a class of men who appear to be as essential in the transaction of daily business, as pen, ink, and paper. In the sunny tropics just as in foggy London, the Broker is a necessity of our daily business life. I am not about to describe the race of fast young vivacius Englishmen who rush frantically round the corners of our streets and suddenly disappear in some merchants' office with all the gasping anxiety born of a Reuter's telegram, stamped on his face. No, I have in my mind a stout, middle-aged party from Jaffna once—from Checkoo Street more recently, in a snow-white turban, marvellously turned-up slippers, and with apparently all the family linen swathed about his middle. Why he came from Jaffna, why he did not hail from Trincomalee or Batticaloa, or even Kaits, I could never quite make out, any more than I could solve the twin problem, why scarcely any but the Jaffnarians are employed as brokers!

Once upon a time, perhaps thirty-five years ago, or suppose we say "the round forty," it was not so. In those primeval times our Broker was one Phillip Saverimuttu, a sort of bamboo of a Canicopully in a ridiculous hat, with peaked corners projecting in front, and a coolie-load of bed-curtain rings in his ears. But these gentry are going out, and with the few exceptions proving the rule, Jaffna reigns supreme in counting-house and bank.

It may not, perhaps, be amiss, if in this place, I indulge in a brief glimpse at history with reference to these two classes of Brokers, so completely distinct and dissimilar. At the early period to which I have already made reference, namely 1837, and indeed, for a dozen years afterwards, the Canicopully class of brokers, cashiers and bill-collectors were alone in the official and commercial world of Colombo. Their ancestors had migrated to Ceylon from the opposite coast of India during the later period of the Portugese rule, as merchants, and were well received by the Europeans, especially by the Dutch, who had a keen eye to business, and saw that these traders were a reliable and most useful class of men. Eventually many of them were employed by the Dutch Government as cashiers in the Custom House, the Treasury and the Commissariat, for the fact of their having embraced the Roman Catholic religion did not stand in their way with the Dutch who were content so long as they employed only Christians.

During the early days of British rule, the Canicopullies, who had never abandoned their occupation as traders, took employment under English merchants, as brokers, and in this capacity continued to act until a comparatively recent period, when they began to be supplanted by another branch of the same caste of Tamils, the Hindoo Tamils of Jaffna, or more properly speaking, of the district of Manipay in the Peninsula of Jaffna: these two, like the Canicopullies, are of the Vellale caste, but of an inferior branch: there are, in fact, several of these, as it is a fact that the Tamils of other districts who never leave their homes in search of employment in Colombo, will not associate with this particular class of migratory Tamils. We are assured that a Tamil from another district, having married the daughter of a Manipay Hindoo, nevertheless had his food cooked, and partook of it separately from his wife. How they arranged with regard to their children I am not informed.

Our original Broker, old Phillip Savarimuttu, performed functions unknown to your modern Jaffnarian: not only was he head cashier, and as such in charge of the strong-room, and of the promissory notes in course of collection, but he was custodian of the godowns and inspector-general of coffee pickers, coolies and bottle washers. When there were no banks to do a discount business, bills were collected in regular course by the Firm, or rather by its Canicopully, and he had for this especial duty a subordinate Canicopully. A great man was Savarimuttu in those days, and when in the spring-tide of the coffee season, with fully three score coffee pickers, at work in the office yard strewn with parchment coffee, with a squall of rain coming on, a dozen chetties taking delivery of piece goods from the godowns, a cart-load of rupees coming in from a Madras vessel, and a French skipper with two or three boxes of sovereigns to be left in exchange for cinnamon and oil, our Broker was in the full blaze and splendour of his glory. It was amusing to see him patronise the Frenchman in Tamil, with his capacious mouth full of betel, bullying the coolies and spluttering at the women, and coaxing the chetties, all in the same breath and with the same set of features: and how, when the day's work was over, and the Firm drove away in the mild family-bandy of the period, he gathered his snowy robes about him like an oriental Roman, and strode solemnly to his stuffy little home in Brassfounder Street.

The brokers of those early days were the sole negotiators between the British merchants and the Chetty dealers of Ceylon, the back bone of native trade.

The Nattucotta Chetties are those to whom I am referring: they came over from the Negapatam district, never for a permanency, usually for a period of five years, at the end of which time their accounts with the firm in South India must be squared up to a point, and no doubtful entries left for their successors to deal with.

One of the most important and probably lucrative branches of the Chetty trade of the olden time has departed from them: they no longer deal in raw cotton, the whole trade in which was transferred to Tuticorin when the cash advance system was abolished: their dealings are now chiefly confined to manufactured cotton goods, rice and coffee: these, at any rate, form their principal articles of trade, and some of them deal in them very largely, to an extent indeed, scarcely conceiveable by those not acquainted with the class. There are some Chetty firms who trade in all these articles, but as a rule the cloth merchants or piece goods Chetties deal in no other articles, whilst rice merchants are generally prepared to traffic in coffee, though as they confine themselves to the native qualities, and these yearly decrease in quantity, their business in this article of produce is on the wane. Of these several descriptions of Chetty firms there are about one hundred and fifty in Colombo, nearly all having branches at Galle, Kandy, Gampola, Badulla, Haldamulle, Ratnapura, and other stations, conducted on the same system as the principal Colombo branches, for the latter Firms are but representatives of or partners in Chetty Houses in Negapatam and elsewhere, and their dealings are regulated by well established custom.

Some of these firms are very wealthy, one Chetty being reported to have out in advances, in rice and cash to planters, as much as £50,000. But we must state that, on the whole, there is not nearly the same amount of capital embarked in the Chetties business in Ceylon as in former days when a large cotton business was done in Colombo : the transference of that business to Tuticorin has shorn the local native trade of much of its old prestige. The Nattucotta Chetties have always carried on business with their own capital, they are not borrowers, on the contrary they lend : they of course discount notes received from purchasers of their goods, but even then not to any great extent. Cautious in the extreme in all their money transactions, they can yet appreciate the sterling qualities of the European merchant and Planters of good standing, and in them they will place unbounded confidence. Men's opinions and feelings necessarily undergo considerable changes with time and circumstances, but we can recall to mind in the days when Banks did not exist in Ceylon, when every merchant had his strong-room in which his supplies of rupees from

Madras were stored, in stout bags containing from £100 to £250 each, duly labelled with tickets bearing the initials of one of the partners: large sums of money were frequently paid away to Chetties for rice from the coast, or for native coffee from the interior, and I can remember when a cart-load of bags of rupees were removed by the Chetty dealer without counting, having implicit faith in the firm's initials. Occasionally the Chetty would at the expiry of a week or so, state that a few rupees were found wanting in one of the bags, upon which the coins were handed over to him without question.

In the good, old fashioned days of which I am writing, and indeed down to a much more recent period, the Chetties, when they made a contract with the merchant for coffee or cotton, invariably received nine-tenths of the value of the cotton and half of the value of the coffee, several months in anticipation of the delivery of the produce. When we add that in their purchases of cotton goods or other British merchandize, they as invariably took all the credit they could get, some idea may be formed of the advantages they possessed in their Ceylon trading operations.

We have likened them to the Israelites, and as buyers and sellers they may well compare with the gentlemen of Duke's Place and Houndsditch. They will haggle for days over a few rupees, but when the bargain is struck, adhere to it with marvellous tenacity. In nearly all merchant's offices there is what is known as "the broker's room," in which the Chetties congregate for gossip, for business, or perhaps for epistolatory purposes. There they prepare such letters as must leave by the afternoon tappal, and they make free use of the pens, ink, and paper of the office for the purpose, so that there is some economy as well as convenience in the use of the broker's room. An incident once occurred in connection with this old established custom of letter writing, strongly illustrative of Chetty character, and which is therefore worth recalling. A well-known Chetty of standing and rather portly presence, in addition to a free use of a certain firm's stationery, used frequently to lounge up to the "Rag" partner, and hold up his addressed letter for a postage stamp, which was of course never refused. But one day, in an evil hour for the British merchant, he ventured to ask his portly Chetty friend, through an interpreter, if he were aware that stationery and postage stamps cost money, did he imagine that merchants obtained them for nothing;—Moona Koona Roona eyed the Britisher for a minute, whilst he scratched his massive shoulders, and then loosening his girdle, took from his pouch and laid on the table an Oriental Bank note for one hundred rupees, and strode haughtily out of the office and up the street. Horrified at the unexpected result of his question, the merchant sent after the Chetty, but Moona Koona was proudly obdurate: he did not receive back the note for many days afterwards, and we believe, was never again as frequently, or as largely a buyer from the firm in question.

That the Nattucotta Chetties should be excellent men of business, need not be matter for surprise, when it is known they are initiated into the mysteries of figures and bargaining from their earliest days: hence the marvellous rapidity and exactness of their calculations, worked out on a simple ola, or dried leaf, with an iron style. The entire caste follow no other occupation than that of traders: they look forward to the business as their inheritance, and accordingly begin life betimes, and in the most humble capacity: a chetty lad, though of wealthy parents, must work his way upwards on the same footing as others, and both in this respect, and in the custom of serving a certain period of their lives in another country, approach very closely to the practice amongst the young traders of Germany. At as early an age as six or seven, they will leave the parental roof and begin life beyond the seas, with one of their neighbours, in the capacity of cook-boy or office-menial. After gaining some experience in the ways of the Chettie world, and becoming tolerably adept at arithmetic, the young apprentice will be promoted to the post of wharf-boy, in which capacity he forms an escort for all goods to and from the Wharf, and at that work will probably remain several years according to his quickness and aptitude. He will then be made salesman to the firm, keeping an account of all goods coming in and going out, and attending to the general dealings of the House. From that position he is raised to the office of assistant accountant, then made an accountant: a year or two more and he will be appointed sub-manager and finally manager, representing often very large interests. Notwithstanding this the highest salary that is generally paid to any of them, is Rs. 1,500 a year, some are in receipt of as little as Rs. 350. As for the subordinates their pay is most insignificant—usually a few rupees, their food, one or two cloths, and a mat. Very little business is done by Chetties in the morning: shortly before noon the manager, his assistant and the accountant will sally forth for the day's work, leaving the salesman and the office boys to attend to buyers: in the evening after sunset, the day's proceedings are posted up in the books, and a regular account made out, and money transactions between one firm and others arranged. It is not a little remarkable that as a rule, Chetties make scarcely any use of Banks for the custody of their money, preferring to retain possession of it themselves, and keeping it in a ponderous chest on which the accountant sleeps at night. This practice arises from no mistrust of the Banks, but from other considerations. They do not care to go to the expense of cheque books when they can pay away their money without charge: again, in the event of death there is no difficulty about drawing out money, there is also their practice of making cash loans to each other for purposes of trade, which is invariably done at night.

Chetties seldom trouble the lawyers, whose services have to be dearly purchased. Nearly all differences amongst themselves are settled by the arbitration of a certain number of the oldest and most experienced of their body, who are called, when thus assembled, a 'Nagaram,' answering to the Bengalee "Punchayet" or the European "Tribunal of Commerce." It is very rarely indeed, that any appeal is ever taken from their decision, which is acted upon at once with most implicit reliance upon its justice. Occasionally it may happen that some headstrong Chettie will refuse to comply with the decision of the 'Nagaram' in which rare case an interdict will be issued forbidding any transaction with the refractory party, who, deprived of all credit or countenance amongst them, is very soon brought to reason. The 'Nagaram' takes cognizance of not only disputes, but offences which are punished by fines paid to one of the two Hindoo Temples in Sea Street, dedicated to the idol "Supermanian." The "Nagaram" is held in one of these temples, or at the office of one of the oldest and wealthiest Chetties.

So much as regards the Colombo Chetties, but alas, for the Saverimuttus and the Anandappas of these latter days, their race is drawing near its end: a rival had appeared on the field, destined at no distant day to supplant them and theirs in the not unlucrative tasks of the counting house and the godown. All the Asiastic invaders of Ceylon have come from the North, and true to historical traditions, Jaffna deputed Muttu Sawmy, the one-eyed, to herald the way for a flight of young Jaffnarians.

How Muttu Sawmy had many years before, settled in Colombo as trader and money lender, and how from small beginnings he had come to be the very Napoleon of Colombo finance, the *friend* of Sir Robert Horton, the necessity of high civilians and their wives, the dispenser of pearls, shawls and official and commercial situations, is it not a matter of history, and did he not import nephews, cousins and sons-in-law, whose name was legion, and from that time have they not with persevering and careful industry, earned for themselves more favor than their old patron's shawls and pearls could ever win?

Now-a-days, although there are still one or two Anandappas lingering about the outskirts of commerce, our Broker is a Manipay Tamil, garbed in flowing robes of purest white and ample turban. Like the Natucotta Chetties, he began life in the most humble capacity—has made himself all that he is.—When a mere boy he came down from the North, just as Dick Whittington walked into London, looking out for the golden paving stones. If he did not discover the precious metal under his feet, he was not long in finding a good deal of dirt, and many odorous cesspits and noxious drains festering in the noon-day sun, round about the crowded home he sought, in Checkoo Street, the house of his father's friend: there he was put under that most useful course of training, learning to exist on the smallest possible modicum of rice and salt fish per diem. How he spent a year in keen observations of all about him, how he was at length started fairly on the high road to fortune by being installed in a merchant's office, or suppose I say in a back verandah in Prince Street, how he performed the important and responsible duties of taking press copies of letters, and listening round corners when bargains were being hatched, and earning kicks for his inquisitiveness, all this is known as matters of family tradition, though it may not be written in the chronicles of young Jaffna.

To-day he is a man of substance, and can undertake to advance loans of startling amount to men of need, having realisable security to offer. Twenty years in the pursuit of cotton and coffee contracts, in the disposal of hundreds of rice cargoes and of many thousands of packages of British manufactures from Manchester, Glasgow and Paisley, all of which brought with them a commission from the Chettie and Singalese dealers, have added greatly to his store, and our broker is now able to make large donations to the temple in Sea Street, to build sundry capacious dwellings for Europeans in the Cinnamon Gardens at a smart rental, to erect a showy residence for himself with a pair of granite elephants to guard the gate-way, and in many ways to earn for himself the regard of British residents and the admiration and envy of indigenous dwellers in Colombo.

When some few years ago, his daughter was married to a swell young broker of the town, was any thing ever known to equal the lavish outlay on those nuptial festivities? Half the civilians, three-fourths of the military and the whole of the mercantile community were invited to grace the festive board with their presence, and many of them graced it. The band of H. M. 150th Regiment was in attendance, though no doubt many of the turban'd guests would have preferred tom-toms, whilst a party of remarkably pretty and extremely naughty Nautch girls twirled round in velvet and silver jackets, and richly embroidered robes to a most suggestive air.

But "our broker" is a very different looking personage to Ramalingam in his daily domesticity. Stretched at full length on a couch never desecrated by the brush of the furniture cleaner of Brassfounder Street, surrounded by a doubtful looking table, and a few ricketty chairs which know not the filth of bees-wax and turpentine, he smokes his early weed in the scantiest of gauzy raiment. There is a sweet simplicity about his homely indigenous life: the crockery is of the plainest, the chippiest and the crackedest: the water from a cocoanut quenches his thirst: his rice cost him little enough, and as for the etceteras, they are supplied by willing and devoted clients who minister to his gastronomic tastes from sheer gratitude in the sense of favors yet to come. The labors of the day over, he can return to the bosom of his family, rather a capacious one by the bye, and sitting in the cool of evening under the shade of the family vine, typified by a group of leafy bananas, and closing his eyes, Phillip dreams the dream of his divinities—commission, interest, and buksheesh.

THE FINE OLD NATIVE GENTLEMAN.

I AM not prepared to assert that the race of fine old Native Gentlemen is extinct: far from it: there are specimens to be met with at the present time, lacking few of the qualities of their ancestors, and in many respects worthy descendants of worthy sires. But altered circumstances, modern education, and a growing indifference towards them on the part of the government, have gradually worked changes in their character. Half a century ago the ancient prestige of the Mudeliyars was unimpaired, and the same remark applies to the Chiefs of the Kandyan district as to those of the Maritime Provinces. There were no brummagem Mudeliyars in those days. Rank was not conferred for the erection of a pandhal, the concoction of an address, or for a few years' service in a provincial Kachcheri. Mudeliyars were in those olden times of the first Singhalese families of the land, and as such were invariably regarded with respect by the people who were ever amenable to their authority. Thus, the fine old Native Gentlemen of bye-gone days were links in the chain which connected the governing with the governed.

Created four centuries ago by the Portuguese rulers of the Maritime provinces, continued with much consideration by the Dutch, and upheld by the early British government, the Mudeliyars were recognised as the nobility of the Singhalese people. In those days a Mudeliyar was the Lord of the Manor, the owner of many broad acres,—a sort of feudal baron of the soil, dwelling in the old paternal mansions, surrounded by an army of retainers who were ready at all times to do his bidding and work his will. That will was, that the people of his district should prosper and be happy. Their interests were his care; and no one, not even the most humble of the poorest villagers, but could approach him and seek his help in time of need.

The "Walauwa" of the Mudeliyar was the audiance hall in which he sat morning and evening to receive and listen to such as came to him with complaints or prayers. There he talked over the affairs of the district with his subordinate headmen, gave orders for work to be executed or tithes to be collected: there he received his friends and chatted for an hour or two each day. His hospitality was as unbounded as his means were ample. His larder was always well-filled with game and fruit, and his cellar with good cheer.

In his home-dress he affected a negligence bordering on the untidy, though his almirahs were full of the richest fabrics from the looms of Holland, in cloth and velvet; and his strong boxes contained the finest diamonds and rubies. On ordinary occasions, he is content with a plain white cambric cloth and loose white coat. The only expensive articles which he affected in daily life were his gold-mounted spectacles, and a jewelled tobacco box, for the Mudeliyar of the olden time indulged in the narcotic leaf. Happy in the possession of wealth beyond what even avarice could covet, he dreamt not of adding to his acres, by those acts of extortion of which we now hear so much. Possessing power and influence, which gave to his merest wish the force of a command, he knew no disappointment, and enjoying honours which if inherited from his fathers, he is equally certain can only descend to his sons, neither jealousies nor rivalries disturbed the easy equanimity of his mind. His sole ambition was to see the honoured name which had come down to him from five generations, perpetuated in his son, and if ever he condescended to ask a favor, it was in connection with this fond aspiration. Hence it was that the history of the last Maha Mudeliyar of the great and noble House of Illangakoon, furnishes an episode containing not a few of the elements of feudal prestige and interest.

It was in about the year 1810, when Governor Sir Thomas Maitland visited the Southern Province, that the Maha Mudeliyar Illangakoon, entertained his Excellency at his mansion near Matara. The spacious dining room was lit in a manner that eye had never till then beheld. The floor was covered with thickest and softest of Dutch carpets, the furniture was of ebony and calamander richly carved and massive withal. The plate was of the purest silver heavily chased, and all, the work of native artists. A hundred servants flitted hither and thither. The luxuries of ice were then unknown, but a large earthenware tank half filled with saltpetre and water did duty for a refrigerator; and dozens of bottles of the choicest Madeira were standing in the cooling liquid. The old Dutch clock, an elaborate work of art itself, struck seven, and the Maha Mudeliyar emerged from an inner chamber, dressed in full court costume: his hair was done up in the usual knot, held by an ample comb of the purest amber coloured tortoise-shell, while a curved comb to match, circumscribed a forehead, the open intellectual breadth of which was displayed to greater advantage by this contrivance. His coat was of the finest broad cloth of marine blue, while the large solid gold buttons that studded it from cuff to waist, and the richly worked "frogs" in place of the ordinary loops, gave to this article of dress a splendour that was dazzling to look upon. The studs, six in number, that buttoned up the shirt-collar and gleamed from his snow-white shirt-front consisted of a single diamond, each of the size of a large pea. The waistcoat buttons that confined the amplitude of a bosom heaving with emotion, were also brilliants of the first water. From his neck dangled a massive chain, to which was attached a medal—a gift to his father from the Dutch Government in recognition of life-long services. The cloth that served for his nether garment, was of the finest cambric and of the purest white, and silk stockings and pumps completed an attire, the *tout ensemble* of which, if wanting in lightness, lacked nothing in ceremonial importance. Immediately a flourish of trumpets announced the arrival of the Governor, the Mudeliyar descended to his portico, and there received the representative of his sovereign, with a dignified yet respectful welcome, removed alike from misplaced familiarity and cringing servility. I

will not to attempt any description of that dinner, the wine that was drunk, or the toasts that were proposed and responded to, but one thing I may note, though calculated to surprise my readers,—that not only was the conversation between host and guest carried on in Portugese, but most of the speeches and the replies were in that language. The dinner at an end, a venerable retainer of the house who had carried the Mudeliyar in his arms as a child, brought in the sole heir of the house of Illangakoon. The happy and proud father presented him to the Governor, who took him on his knee, and after speaking a few kind words, placed him on the table. The Governor rose and at the same time the assembled guests stood up: he made a short address full of compliments to the host, and expressive of the hope that the little boy before them would grow up in health and strength, and worthily maintain the ancestral honors of his house. The family sword and the rich lace belt were then handed to the Governor, who proceeded to invest the boy of scarce seven years with the rank and insignia of Mudeliyar of the Morowak Korle. Three British cheers hailed the newly-made Mudeliyar; glasses were filled all round, and his health drunk in brimming bumpers. That boy-mudeliyar was in due course sent to the seminary at Colombo, where he acquired the knowledge that was to qualify him for the position he was destined to fill. His salary in the meantime was regularly paid, and accumulated into a respectable sum by the time he attained to manhood and went back to take up the Mudeliyarship. Before the good old man was gathered unto his fathers, he had the satisfaction of seeing his son rise to the *Attepattu* Mudeliyarship. That son too lived to a good old age, and left his name, his wealth, and his honours to his son, who, not unworthily, perpetuates the glories of their house as Mudeliyar of the Belligam Korle and Mudeliyar of the Governor's Gate; and so long as nobility of birth, combined with much personal worth continue to evoke a sentiment of regard, may the illustrious house of Illangakoon never want an heir in whom those virtues are reflected! But the civilization of the day, and other circumstances are fast unloosing those ties which bound the people to their hereditary Chiefs. A little knowledge, a little influence, and a little favour, are now the three essentials of a Mudeliyar.

Not longer than thirty years ago the Governor of Ceylon made it his special care that once a-year at least, the native Chiefs of the maritime and mountain provinces were bidden to his halls to partake of the liberal hospitality of their sovereign's representative. There, after witnessing the mazy dance, supper was served for the Chiefs in one long hall, radient with light and hung with trophies and emblems of their native land. The Governor walked amongst them, held converse with one and the other, and before leaving the festive hall stood at one end of the centre table and proposed the health of their Queen, responded to with hearty loyalty. This good old custom is observed no longer. A quarter of a century has passed away since Kandyan and Low country Chiefs were thus bidden to the festive board, and we must not wonder that they feel the slighting neglect. We must cease to marvel how it has happened that there is no longer the same feeling, the same public spirit amongst them; that few of them preserve their ancient prestige, and that too often the decendents of the old feudal lords of the soil, fall into habits that destroy alike their influence and their self-respect.

Not alone in the neglect of former hospitalities towards them do the native Chiefs of Ceylon find their prestige lowered: they complain, and with good reason, of penniless boys, cutcherry clerks, or low-caste adventurers basking in the favor of indiscreet officials, thrust into the responsible office of Korle Mudeliyar, to the destruction of all respect and the subversion of all discipline within the district. How this mistaken disregard of native usages affects the relations of one headman with another may be imagined, when I tell how a Mohandiram or inferior headman, has been known to receive the Mudeliyar, his chief, seated, whilst the latter felt compelled to stand in the presence of the inferior officer of a higher caste.

HULFSDORP.

IT is one of England's proudest boasts that wherever her flag is unfurled, wherever her supremacy is established, there she carries the blessings of liberal institutions: she conquers but to set free. The same justice which is provided for the proudest son of Albion, is sent forth across the waters to attend on the meanest swarthy subject of Her Majesty, in distant India. At the same time, this beautiful feature of our constitution, admirably as it reads on paper, excellent as it sounds to the ear, but too frequently fails in its mission of mercy; and, in one way, or the other, proves rather the reverse of an unmitigated blessing to those for whose special benefit it was wafted over the seas. In India proper, the way to justice, open though it is intended to be, becomes so overgrown with rank bribery and extortion, that the poor Ryot has small chance of passing the threshold: the very attempt to do so subjects him to cruel, relentles persecution. In other places, Ceylon amongst the rest, matters are widely defferent: here, so broad and open is the highway to the law, that none are shut out from it; but unfortunately, the Singhalese are fond of disputation in every shape: having a dislike for action, they make up the deficiency in talk: in addition to which, their innate love of importance is gratified by the reflection that for their sake, and at their instance, the "great Europe master," as they term the judge, is busily occupied, books and all included, for days together. So powerful has this Singhalese passion for litigation become, that it is matter of notoriety, in this country, that legal proceedings are instituted in cases involving no greater stake than the one-fourth part of a cocoanut tree, or the sixteenth share of a sterile paddy field. Nor are these the worst features in this state of things: the litigious spirit begets a host of evil passions in family circles, leading not unfrequently to acts of violence and even bloodshed. So strongly has this passion for law taken hold of the native population that there are very few Singhalese who will not willingly risk their little all to carry some frivolous point against a neighbour, or a near and dear relation. This state of society has raised up a race of harpies of the law, whose name is truly legion, who thrive on the follies of the litigants, and who too frequently fan the slumbering embers into a blazing flame.

Of all the strange scenes which in the East strike a new comer with their novelty, few appear so remarkable as a Singhalese court of justice. There is in it such an odd jumble of western and eastern life, of European forms and oriental fashions, that the beholder, gazing on the scene for the first time, feels rather at a loss to know if he be in a court of law, at a mock auction, or at a debating club.

The Criminal Sessions were on at Colombo with a rather smart sprinkling of cases for the judge, who was sitting in the tribunal, situated outside the fort, at some little distance. The origin of these Courts being removed from the precincts of the fort is curious. It is said that during the Dutch sway in Ceylon, when the Supreme Court held its sitting within the fortified walls of Colombo, an attempt was made by the then governor, Rip Van-something, to overawe the judges in some cases in which he was officially interested, whereupon they claimed from their High Mightinesses of the Netherlands the privilege of holding session without the walls, which was granted, and has been continued ever since.

A ride to the Courts at Hulfsdorp, overlooking the long busy town of Colombo, is by no means a pleasant affair on a hot, choking day during the dry weather. The red, scorching dust blinds and burns one like so much quicklime. The stench from many a dried up ditch and stagnant drain blends harmoniously with the effluvia from the bazaar around, where fish and meat blister and blacken in the burning sun, while files of dozing oily natives lay steaming upon heaps of filth, adding their own unclean aroma to the hot sickly atmosphere.

The neighbourhood is dense, teeming with dirt and children. The coffin-makers are driving a roaring trade; especially one by the arrack tavern, for half the folks round the corner died the night previously of putrid fish, sour pine-apples, and stagnant drains, and the other half were expected to die on the next day. I urged my sorry hack on at the top of his speed, fully five miles an hour, past the crazy old Dutch houses and the dusty, tumble-down Moormen's dwellings, up the steep hill, on the brow of which stood a whole colony of buildings large and small, old and new. This spot was Hulfsdorp, whence, in days long past, the Dutch army which besieged ancient Colombo—then in the hands of the Portuguese, —poured a storm of shot upon the fortifications. It was, afterwards, the country residence of the Dutch governor, the present Supreme Court-House having been tenanted by a long line of sovereign Mynheers. The spot is pleasant enough after the dreadful streets below, commanding a fine view over the fort to seaward, and enjoying an occasional breeze, when there is any. A portion of the great triangular block of buildings around the green, facing the road, is devoted to the Supreme Court, another part to the District Court, and a third to the Police Court, and sundry offices of Record. Around and about this pile of law has sprung up a busy mass of quaint, queer-looking edifices of all shapes, styles and sizes. These are the houses of business of the fraternity of proctors, Dutch, Portuguese, Tamil, and Singhalese, who, if they, as some malicious people say, be really inflicted on the natives as a chastisement for their sins, do their best to fulfil their mission. Each doorway was choked up by hungry applicants for law: groups of litigants squatted beneath the clumps of dusty bananas in the little stony court-yard in front, counting up their witnesses as commercial articles, not for export it is true, but for home use, and are valued by a well-understood sliding-scale. A witness in a murder case, if he be a stout swearer, costs five rix-dollars; in a land suit, witnesses may be had for two or three dollars; burglary or cattle-stealing witnesses are cheaper, they cost about a dollar each; whilst a few copper coins will obtain all the swearing you want and something over, in an ordinary assault case.

I hastened on, past all these scenes, to the Supreme Court, whose labor was just commencing for the day. The court house wherein sat the Puisne Justice in criminal sessions, was a long rambling shed of a place, not unlike a paved barn with a tiled roof. Making my way into the body of the Court I found it filled with the representatives of almost every nation in the eastern hemisphere, blended with Dutch, Portuguese, and English. I might have taken it for a masquerade by day-light were it not for the Court on the little raised stage at one end, with the dirty lion and unicorn, and the figure of Justice looking quite knocked up by the climate. The judge wore a very comical appearance in spite of his gravity. Seated upon an open platform on a level with our faces, I could see plainly enough, as he crossed his legs, that he wore high-lows which required mending, with queer-looking worsted socks.

In a ricketty sort of sheep-pen on one side sat the jury —a motley blending of several nationalities. The fore-man was studying the coat of arms over the judge's head, wondering when the lion and unicorn would finish fighting for the crown. The rest of the jurors were either dozing or amusing themselves in the best way they could. Opposite the jury was a large parrot's cage without any top; this was the witness-box. Further away there was another parrot cage, in which the crier of the court tried to keep order by creating more noise than all the disturbers put together.

Grouped about a shabby-looking ale-house table, covered with a rusty cloth of some impossible colour, were the

European auditory and some three or four barristers and proctors, the former of mixed races, the latter native.

An important case was on: a native was being tried for murder and the court was crowded to suffocation. The prisoner, a haggard, broken-spirited man, was docked opposite the judge, and glanced in a wild, frightened manner, from his counsel to the Court, and then to the jury, wondering what it all meant; he had confessed his guilt, and why need they take so much trouble with him? The counsel for the prisoner was on his legs about to say something; he was a European, a hale, portly, bold man, with a twinkling, cunning eye and a shining face. I was rather at a loss to know if he were going to make a speech, or sing a comic song, but it ended in his challenging the best part of the jurors—the best part in every sense, for when he sat down, the foreman, who had been studying the lion and unicorn so deeply and all his fellow Europeans had disappeared, replaced by others of a kindred hue with the prisoner.

It was a long and tedious affair, that trial, despite the man's confession, and as all the intricate native evidence had to be translated and re-translated, I soon grew tired of the scene, and bent my steps towards the minor courts close by. Between the two localities were long dusty verandahs opening into little dens of offices, were 1 saw through the dirty barred windows, a strange collection of mouldy wooden cupboards, ricketty desks and armless old chairs: heaps of dusty papers were there too, and with them smoke-dried natives redolent of heat and the dirt, as though they were convicted criminals —Singhalese lawyers condemned for their enormous crimes to toil for the rest of their lives over perplexing suits and ghost-like documents. There were deputy-registrars, and translators, and process clerks, and a host of other legal subordinates, caged up like wild beasts at a fair. How different from the vicinity of the law courts at home! There, everything is cool, solemn, silent, orderly; here, it is all glaring sunshine, dirt noise, dust, and effluvia. The very pariah dogs curl up their sickly noses and scamper hastily past.

Forcing my way through a mob of rather moist Malabars and steaming Singhalese, I reached the District Court, where the provincial judge sits all the year round in civil jurisdiction. The court-yard in front, the enclosed space in the rear, the filthy verandahs at the two ends, all were densely studded with anxious groups of natives, smoking, talking, drinking, quarrelling, crying. Under the gloomy shade of some bread-fruit trees, were ranged many members of some Singhalese family who had evidently travelled from a far-off village, to be present at the hearing of their case.

Out rushed a peon from the crowded court, and bawling out some dreadfully singular name, he rushed back again as suddenly as though he just remembered having left all his earthly treasures within reach of those hungry lawyers, and there was no time to be lost. The family group watched the summoned witness as he disappeared amidst the army of suitors at the doorway, envying him the brief importance he was about to assume in open court.

Around the entrances to this crowded seat of justice, were wedged in compact masses, scores of curious and anxious listeners. Amidst that crowd of Singhalese, Moors, Malays, Tamils, and many other races, I observed an old woman seated by the lintal on the brick floor, grasping with clasped hands some curious little bunch of leaves and flowers; and as she rocked her body to and fro, muttering half aloud some wordy jumble, I observed that she cast her eyes at intervals upon a tall, young man, her son doubtless, who, raised above the crowd, could both see and hear what was passing in court. Their case was then on, and the man was evidently telegraphing to her the progress of the suit. The bunch of flowers in her hands was a Buddhist charm, given by their village priest to ensure success. I failed, however, in ascertaining the value of the case. The last witness was not needed. The judge summed up but briefly; there was a momentary silence in that Babel-place, the assessors concurred—the old woman ceased to rock herself she dropped the flower-charm, it was an evil omen to do that; a busy hum in court told all was over; the dark scowl on the tall man's brow needed no interpretation, he sprang down from his elevated perch, and ran to the poor old woman. She had fallen down in a fit, and lay apparently motionless on the pavement.

My dress and colour obtained for me an entrance within the doors, and after a time, a seat near the bench, whence I could watch the proceedings, and note the many strange actors. Perched in a rather roomy, but low pulpit, the judge was listening to the opening of a fresh case from a young but leading proctor, who leant over with his elbow resting on his Honour's desk in the most familiar manner imaginable, just as one might be discussing the state of the weather or the quality of yesterday's dinner. A long table was before "the Court" at a short distance, at which were seated the "Colombo Bar," a motley gooup and curious to look on. They were Dutch Portugese, Tamil and Singhalese: some were steady-going business-like men, and some were very sharp gentry indeed, especially one little parched fellow with close cropped hair and careworn features: but there were several whom you could not, by any imaginative faculty, connect with the Bar. One curious object, out at elbows, leant listlessly over the dirty table, staring at the sparrows up in the roof, whilst another briefless member of the fraternity amused himself by emptying the contents of an inkstand into his neighbour's pocket.

The case then on, though one of very common occurrence, seemed to me a rather prepossessing one, from the fact of its being a question of a bond debt: a suit which, however easily to be settled by actual documentary proof, nevertheless afforded ample scope for a vast deal of very hard Singhalese swearing on both sides, and, of course, in precisely opposite directions. It involved a rather smart amount for a native to meet, not less than one hundred and twenty-two pounds British currency; I'm afraid to say how much it was in the benighted coin of the island, but more than I should like to count. Well, the plaintiff swore as hard as a curry-stone, that the defendent owed the money, and the defendant vowed rather harder, I thought, that he did not owe so much as a single copper-challie. Plaintiff chuckled all over as he produced the defendant's bond for the precise amount. It was examined and conned over, and looked at in all possible ways by every one interested, until at last the judge was on the point of deciding as a matter of course, when the defendant produced a document very similar in appearance and handed it to the judge. It was a release in full for the amount, duly signed by the plaintiff, and as duly witnessed.

Never shall I forget the strange look of humbled mortification and disappointed rage visible in the plaintiff's face, nor the glow of merry bursting triumph that puckered up the oily countenance of the successful defendant. The case was suddenly made as clear one way as the moment before it had been equally lucid. The judge decided against the plaintiff with all the costs and a severe lecture; which, as it afterwards appeared, he deserved from a far more serious point of view than was at the time believed. I was a good deal puzzled at the stupidity of the man who could thus bring an action for a debt of which he had granted a discharge; but the puzzle was cleared up a day or two afterwards, when I learnt all the particulars from the proctor for the defendant in the matter.

The lawyer had been waited upon in his office by his client in the bond case, who came to thank him for the trouble he had taken in conducting his defence. After a few introductory civilities, the proctor congratulated his native friend on the success which had attended him in his recent suit, and remarked on the great necessity that existed for carefully preserving all documents relating to cash transactions, especially such as bore reference to property. The Singhalese looked at his lawyer very hard, with a peculiar expression of deep cunning stealing over his sable countenance. He drew his chair somewhat nearer to him and glancing cautiously round the room to ascertain if any one was within ear-shot, told him in a low half-whisper, that he "had never paid the money." The proctor, as may easily be imagined, was astounded at this admission, although from his long acquaintance with the native character he was generally prepared to hear a good deal of rascality and duplicity. He begged his client to explain what he meant; how he came by the discharge which the plaintiff had not attempted to disprove or set aside, if, as he said he had not paid the money.

The late defendant drew still more confidently near to his lawyer's seat, looking him steadily in the face, as if to watch the effect his communication would have on him, he whispered in his ear that he had not only never paid plaintiff the mony in dispute, but that he had never owed him the amount, nor any sum of money whatever! This was a fearful staggerer to the lawyer, who looked all sorts of questions at his client. The latter perceiving that his riddle was not likely to be solved without his own assistance, condescended to detail every particular relating to the recent suit. He had been on bad terms, he said with the plaintiff, who was a neighbour, for some months past, owing to his having obtained a judgment against the latter in a trifling land case. The plaintiff had been heard to say, that he would one day be revenged on him, and the Singhalese are tolerably true to their word in all these matters, the attempt was expected. The revenge taken was to forge a bond from the defendant to plaintiff for such an amount as must have effectually ruined the former; the deed was well drawn up, properly attested and duly witnessed by men who, for a rupee a head, were in court for the purpose, and actually did swear to the genüineness of defendant's signature. The man would assuredly have been ruined as was intended, but that he happened to be as clever a rogue and as unscrupulous as his adversary. He had heard the old proverb about sharp instruments cutting two ways, and acted upon it, for he concocted a forged discharge to the forged bond, signed by twice as many witnesses as the bond itself, and some of whom were the same parties who professed to have witnessed the execution of the latter and who, for a little higher bribing, came into court to swear by the sacred tooth of Buddha, that they had seen the plaintiff sign and deliver the discharge! The Proctor went home that day a wiser man by a great deal, than when he entered his little office in the morning, and deeply impressed with the difficulties flung round the path of justice by the crookedness of the native character.

Having related the *denouement* of the above little plot, I must terminate my day at the Colombo courts. After the decision of the case just alluded to, I bent my steps back to the Supreme Court, which was at that moment in a state of intense commotion. It was evident that something of great interest had happened; for every tongue was in action, every bare arm was flung about as though there had been a general attack of St. Vitus's dance amongst the native population. Great white eyes glared fiercely on their neighbours; black hair streamed over excitable, oleaginous shoulders; muslin turbans and snow-white scarfs danced about, and blended madly with Turkey-red cloths and chintz sarongs; bloodthirsty-looking moustachoes curled to their uttermost tips in rank defiance, while tobacco and betel-juice flew about in copious showers, and much nearer to me than I could have desired. What did it all mean? Was the poor wretch of a murderer, self-condemned as he had been, about to suffer the extreme penalty of the law, then and there, on the spot, just to give dame Justice an appetite for her afternoon meal! I ventured to question a respectable-looking man by my side, in clean, white raiment; but the poor creature muttered something that might have been Ethiopic or Sclavonic. I tried a thin weazen-faced old man in spectacles and cloth garments, and the oddity replied in Portugese!

Forcing my way into the body of the court, I at length ascertained from a half-caste proctor, that although the prisoner had pleaded guilty, and the evidence and summing-up of the judge were dead against him, the jury had acquitted the man. They knew far better than he did whether he was or was not guilty, and in their wisdom had decided that he was mistaken in his self-condemnation. The prisoner—the prisoner no longer—could not be persuaded that he heard aright; when I reached the thronged table facing the dock, I found him staring vacantly about him, with his long, bony hands clasped firmly together; the person in charge of him in vain tried to move him from the spot. The officials were conversing together in deep, earnest whispers, evidently as astonished as the poor creature they had just being trying; after a brief time they dismissed the jury, having probably had sufficient of their labour for that day, and for many days to come; and eventually the court rose and adjourned over until the following morning, to allow themselves time to digest their astonishment.

As I drove home from witnessing these strange scenes, I could not resist pondering upon the crooked ways of orientals; upon the dim moral perceptions of our fellow-subjects in the East. I called to mind the hackneyed Exeter Hall phrase of "We are all brethren," and thought how much better for the true advancement of the human family it would be, if, whilst admitting the abstract truth of the above sentence, men paused a while ere working out the theory by one universal rule of legislation; if they would bear in mind that there "is a season for all things." Such worldly-wise philanthropists have yet to learn that in regard to their "we-are-all-brethren" idea, what is "sauce for the goose," is not always "sauce for the gander."

THE CINNAMON PEELER.

OVER the boisterous ocean, steam-borne for many a stormy day to where the white man trades on sunny shores, over the burning plains, across the cloud-capped ranges, and then once more into the plains where slaves delve in the bowels of the earth for precious metals, the bales of spice are borne, and the long string of mules leave their rich burthens. On stormy seas of snow-clad lands; across dessert tracks within the distant Russian town where the grand pinnacle of a Greek church rears its solemn front: soft trains of melody ascend within the sacred pile and the rich streams of incense rise from many an altar. In the orange grove just off the Plaza, where the grass is thick and soft, and the orange blossom lends its fragrance to the sweet air of southern Spain, a group of laughing damsels seated on the velvet sward, sip their tiny cups of chocolate, and pour out their little stores of scandal.—Down in a dark, dank cellar-looking vaulted space, a mill-stone moves steadily, unwearedly; no motive power is seen, but a grim-looking silent man in leather apron, armed with a giant brush and heavy rod, tends to the mash of substances crushing beneath the stone, into fine powder, almost impalpable.

Into all of these, into the powder ground for "Thorley's Cattle Food", into the tiny cup of chocolate, sipped by young Spanish damsels, into the incense on the altar, into the daily drink within the fever-sticken depths of quicksilver mines, our own special spice enters a part of the composition. Steamers are freighted with it, mules are laden with it, droskies are filled with it, waggons and vans are piled and heaped with it, until it has become hard to say how much of it is a necessary, and how much a luxury.

Well may Spaniard, Russian, or Mexican dream of the sunny land where grows this precious spice, as a bright spot on earth, green, fresh and tropically radiant, teeming with vegetable and insect life, where in the far off, olden, scriptural times, gallies were freighted with ivory, apes and peacocks,—with pearls, and spice, and perchance, with gold of Ophir.

But who, and what, and where are the oriental workers who produce this precious spice? Are they rich or poor, honored or spurned, exalted or debased, free or slave? Within a low-roofed shed in which to enter though not of lofty stature, one must stoop, a row of silent, half-clad, half-fed, quarter-washed, dark-skinned workers are seated on the ground, plying a curious little knife which scrapes and scatters the outer cuticle from long, half-round strips of young sapling bark. These pieces are the cinnamon bark removed from the ripe sticks on the previous day, left in a pile to undergo a sort of semi-fermentation, and when scraped clean and sorted carefully, and trimmed scientifically, and packed and piped delicately, one within the other, to the extent of three or four, according to the thinness of the quill, or the fancy of the quiller, they become the famed cinnamon of Ceylon, unique in its quality, unrivalled in it production. Other countries have essayed to grow it,—Java, China, India, Manilla,—and for aught we know, other countries, have started as rivals in the culture, but from cause of soil, or climate, or cultivation, or all, failure has been the final ending, and to this day Ceylon is the sole country of the fragrant spice.

It was no doubt, owing to the presence of this precious spice in quantities along the western sea-borde, not less than the rich fertility of the country, which induced the early European adventurers to fix on this harborless side of the island, for a trading settlement, instead of in the vicinity of Trincomalie with its miles of bays and inland waters, wherein all the navies of the world might ride at anchor. The spice was, however, but seldom seen in Europe, so scarce and costly was it. Scattered in uncertain quantities along the sea-coast, and in some of the jungles and chena lands of the interior, it was in those early days, and even up to the Dutch time, collected chiefly in payment of tribute from the Kandyans, or in lieu of taxes by the low-country Singhalese. No cultivation of the plant was then attempted, nor was it even brought together or preserved in special localities until a century later, when the Dutch, keenly alive to their interests in all commercial matters, took to cinnamon cultivation, if that name could be applied to mere clearing out of masses of plants, keeping down low jungle, and draining the ground from stagnant water. That this was all that could have been done by the Dutch Government, is evident from the records of the cinnamon department of those days.

But there was yet another reason for this cultivation being preferred to the old method of collection. Their frequent warfare with the Kandyans rendered it often difficult and sometimes impossible to procure the quantity needed to make up their bi-annual shipments to Europe, hence it became a matter of policy to secure a supply quite independently of that hitherto gathered in the Kandyan jungles.

The cultivation of the spice in the present time, is carried on by labor of any description, but the operation of peeling is with but few exceptions, in the hands of the chalias, or as they were termed under the Dutch, the "mahabadde," derived from the words "great tax," the chalia people having been compelled to pay a heavy tax to the government in prepared cinnamon. In the present day, whilst they are free from the tribute, they are deprived of the many privileges enjoyed by their ancestors, being paid for the results of their labor at certain understood rates which are sufficiently productive, when a man is expert and has a wife and one or two children to assist him : villages in the Galle district are the places of residence of large numbers of peelers, but they have been much scattered since 1833 when the monopoly in the spice trade was abolished. In those palmy days the cinnamon peelers had their own headmen, and could be tried for an offence only by their European superintendent, a Government official who was sworn in as magistrate of the "mahabadde." Now, the peeler is but one of the common multitude, amenable to the ordinary courts, and obliged to be content with four or five pounds British currency at the end of the cinnamon harvest, with which, and the produce of the fraction of a field, and a miserable fenceless garden, he has to do his best to pay for rice, a few common cloths, and a little salt-fish, curry-stuff, and oil. Take him when you will, the peeler never presents a cheerful exterior, his dress and bearing give no outward token of prosperity; the unwashed cloth and uncombed hair tell eloquently of the daily struggle that is going on with the demon want, and even on holidays he and his belongings cut but sorry figures, amidst the genial gatherings of the village community.

There is no doubt that the abolition of rajakaria and the privileges of the "mahabadde," have not bettered the condition of the cinnamon peelers. In the early days of British rule he was wont to receive from the Government two-thirds of a measure of rice daily, with a measure of salt per month, and subsistence money at the rate of three pence a day, besides freedom from tolls, ferries, &c., in consideration of which he was bound to deliver 80 lbs. to 100 lbs. of cinnamon properly prepared. After the abolition of this system, the Government paid them according to the quantity and quality of the spice delivered, 5½d., 5d., and 4½d. per pound. But the rate now is much lower, and when the exactions of the canganies and petty headmen have been satisfied, there is not more than the sum we have mentioned with which to support their families. But even this amount is far more than is ever touched by large numbers of cultivators: the peeler is, however, an improvident man: migrating from his village for months in the year, and herding with numbers of others in the estate "lines," he falls into improvident, thoughtless ways, indulges in frequent potations, and when at length he returns to his village with his hard-earned but greatly reduced stock of coin, he has lost much of his inclination for work: he turns to his field and his garden with stolid indifference, and by the time his cash has nearly melted away, he finds the season for cultivation almost over, the field bearing abundant crops of weeds, and the garden overgrown with brambles. He sighs heavily as he sees the necessity for action in the reduced size of his rice bag. Work for hire, he will not: he may perchance go out on a fishing bout, or he may insist on the wife and children beating out some coir husks, if he be in the Galle district, and with the fibre he may work up a pingoe-load or two of coir yarn in order to barter it for tobacco and food, but anything like sustained industry is altogether foreign to the dreamy nature of the cinnamon peeler.

ELEPHANTS, AND HOW TO CATCH THEM.

THE elephant is associated with my earliest recollections of school-boyhood. Well do I remember the huge black picture of the unwieldy animal in Mavor's Spelling Book, the letter-press describing the creature as "not only the largest, but the strongest of all quadrupeds," which is beyond all question; and furthermore, that "in a state of nature, it is neither fierce nor mischievous;" which is the very reverse of fact, as hundreds of sugar and coffee planters, as well as many a traveller, could testify. In later years, I enjoyed a peep at the sleepy-looking creature, cooped up in a sort of magnified horse-stall, at the Zoological Gardens, in the Regent's Park, and well I remember wondering how so much sagacity and thoughtfulness could be attributed to so apathetic and cumbrous an animal.

The reader of Roman and Grecian history may gather how Pyrrhus for a time mastered the hardy veterans of Rome, by means of these then little-known and terrible creatures; and how Alexander found hundreds of them opposed to him in the army of the Indian monarch. Readers of more recent history may learn how these animals formed a portion of the vast armies of most of the Indian Nabobs, with which the British forces came in contact. But twelve short months ago, the elephant graced the civic triumph of the newly-elected Lord Mayor of London, to the unmitigated astonishment and delight of thousands of little boys and elderly females.

Much, however, as I had heard and read of the elephant, I never properly appreciated this animal, until I had been a dweller in Eastern lands where I was witness of such performances by these huge creatures, that my feeling towards them was raised from that of mere wonder, to something more akin to respect and admiration.

In the course of my early morning rides about the vicinity of Colombo, I frequently reined in my steed to watch the quiet labours of a couple of elephants in the service of the Government. These huge animals were generally employed in the Commissariat timber-yard, or the Civil Engineer's department, either in removing and stowing logs and planks, or in rolling about heavy masses of stone for building purposes. I could not but admire the precision with which they performed their allotted task, unaided, save by their own sagacity. They were one morning hard at work, though slowly, piling up a quantity of heavy pieces of timber; the lower row of the pile had been already laid down, with mathematical precision, six logs side by side. These they had first pushed in from the adjoining wharf; and, when I rode up, they were engaged in bringing forward the next six for the second row in the pile. It was curious to observe those uncouth animals seize one of the heavy logs at each end, and, by means of their trunks, lift it up on the logs already placed, and, then arrange it crosswise upon them with the most perfect skill. I waited whilst they thus placed the third row; feeling a curiosity to know how they would proceed when the timber had to be lifted to a greater height. Some of the logs weighed about twelve hundred-weights. There was a short pause before the fourth row was touched; but the difficulty was no sooner perceived than it was overcome. The sagacious animals selected two straight pieces of timber, placed one end of each piece on the ground with the other resting on the top of the pile so as to form a sliding way for the next logs; and, having seen that they were perfectly steady and in a straight line, the four-legged labourers rolled up the slope they had thus formed, the six pieces of timber, for the fourth layer on the pile. Not the least amusing part of the performance was, the careful survey of the pile made by one of the elephants, after placing each log, to ascertain if it were laid perfectly square with the rest.

The sagacity of these creatures in detecting weakness in the jungle-bridges thrown across some of the streams in Ceylon, is not less remarkable. I have been assured that when carrying a load, they invariably press one of their fore-feet upon the earth-covering of the bridge to try its strength; and, that if it feels too weak to carry them across, they will refuse to proceed until lightened of their load. On one such occasion a driver persisted in compelling his elephant to cross a bridge against the evident wish of the animal; and, as was expected by his comrades, the rotten structure gave way, elephant and rider were precipitated into the river, and the latter was drowned.

Having thus been much prepossessed in favor of these docile creatures, I learnt with considerable interest in the latter part of the year 1849, that an elephant kraal was in preparation, in the Western Province of Ceylon, not many miles from Colombo.

The word kraal signifies simply a trap; inasmuch as the wild elephants are caught by partly driving, and partly enticing them within a large enclosed space, or trap. It is assuredly much safer sport than elephant shooting, and generally attracts a large number of spectators. I may here mention that in spite of the scholastic authority of Mavor's Spelling Book, the wild elephants of Ceylon are far from being "neither fierce nor mischievous." At times they descend upon the low country from their mountain fastnesses in such numbers and with such ferocity, as to carry with them destruction, and often death. Elephant kraals are, therefore, resorted to for the double purpose of ridding a neighbourhood of these dangerous visitors, and supplying the Government with fresh beasts of labour for their timber-yards and building establishments. On these occasions the natives of the district turn out *en masse* —from the rich Mudeliyar to the poorest cooly—to assist without remuneration; all being interested in the success of the affair.

The whole province was alive with excitement: nothing was talked of at mess-table, or at Government House, but the approaching kraal. Half Colombo, it was said, would be there; and, as the weather promised to be so fair, I could not resist the temptation to witness the trapping of a score or two of those unruly monsters of the forest.

Such excursions are always undertaken by parties of three or more, for the sake of comfort. I joined four friends for the occasion; two gentlemen, and two ladies, mother and daughter. They were well acquainted with the Government Agent of the locality, who had promised them shelter, and good accommodation for witnessing the kraal. All arrangements having been completed, our servants gaily turbaned, accompanied by a swarm of coolies, bearing provisions, bedding, and other comforts, started off one fine moon-light night; and, at a little before day-break on the following morning, we followed them on the road; the ladies in a small pony-chaise, and myself and friend on our nags. Long before nightfall we reached the village adjoining the scene of sport. We needed no guide to the locality, for the narrow road was crowded with travellers hastening in one direction. Every description of vehicle lined the way; from the Colonel's light tandem, to the native bullock hackery, with its ungreased, squeaking wheels.

The scene at the village was singularly strange and exciting. It was close to the banks of the Calany, a river of some size and rapidity. Along the palm-shaded shore were moored numberless boats; many of them large flat country barges, or padé boats, containing parties of visitors from Colombo, who had prudently determined to take up their abode in those floating residences for the night. The village huts had been thrown open to the English visitors after having been well cleaned and white-washed. Their doors were gaily ornamented with strips of red and white cloth, flowers, and the fresh pale-green leaves of the cocoa-palm. When the little cottages were lit up for the evening, they looked extremely pretty.

It was at once evident that there was not nearly sufficient accommodation for all the guests. One of our party started in search of his friend, the Government Agent, but in vain; he had gone off in quest of the elephants, reported to be coming up fast from the neighbouring dense jungles. Consequently we were left to our own resources. After some delay, we succeeded in obtaining the use of one small room for the ladies; whilst, for ourselves, we sought shelter for the night beneath the friendly and capacious roof of one of the Padé boats, where we found a hearty welcome from a party of young rollicking coffee-planters.

Day had not appeared next morning when we were afoot: and, having sipped a cup of vile, half-boiled coffee, we started to explore the wonders of the kraal; followed, of course, by our servants, with sundry tin boxes and a hamper.

The neighbourhood in which the kraal was formed, consisted of rugged undulating ground pretty thickly covered with stout jungle. Heavy, low forest trees studded the stony land, interwoven with thorny brambles, cacti, bamboos, and a species of gigantic creeping plant, called, appropriately, jungle-rope, for it is strong enough to bind the stoutest buffalo that ever roared. A number of narrow paths had been cut through the jungle leading from the village to the kraal. Through one of these winding, prickly tracks, we bent our slow way, seeing little around us save hugely-branched trees and thickly-matted underwood. Half-an-hour's walk brought us to a halt. We were at the kraal. I looked around; but, the only indications of the industry of man in that wild spot, were sundry covered platforms, raised amongst the leafy branches of trees, some twelve feet from the ground. These places contained seats, and were already filling with visitors; we followed the example, and mounting the rude staircase, obtained a good view of what was going on. Before us lay a large open space, in extent about two acres, irregular in shape, and of very uneven surface. A few stout trees were standing at intervals within it; beside which were to be seen groups of natives carrying long white wands, for all the world like so many black stewards of some public dinner or ball. Around this plot of ground grew a wall of dense jungle; and, on looking into this, I perceived that it had been made artificially strong by intertwining amongst it the heavy trunks of trees, long bamboos, and jungle-rope of enormous thickness. At first sight, this natural wall did not appear to be anything more than ordinary jungle; such as might easily be forced by any ordinary village buffalo. We were, however, assured by the native master of the ceremonies, the head Korale, that this jungle would resist the fiercest attacks of the strongest Kandian elephant. At one end of the enclosure I perceived a narrow opening, partly covered with light brambles and branches of trees. This was the entrance to the kraal; so arranged as to wear a natural appearance. Besides this carefully concealed gateway were hidden a number of active villagers, ready prepared with huge trunks of trees and jungle-rope; with which they were to secure the passage against any attempts at return, so soon as the elephants were trapped.

The novelty of our situation; the wild solitude of jungle around us; the picturesque appearance of the many groups of natives within and about the kraal; the stories of elephant shooting and trapping, and narrow escapes, with sundry references to portly baskets and boxes of provisions; all helped to make the day pass away rapidly and comfortably enough. Evening, however, brought with it a general debate as to what should be done; for there were still no signs of game being near; and few of us desired to spend the night in that open spot, unless uuder a strong inducement. The discussion ended by an adjournment to the village and the Padé boat, where we slept soundly.

The following day was spent pretty much as had been the first. Some of the visitors gave strong signs of impatience; and towards evening, a few, of worse temper than the rest, declared the whole affair a complete take in, and took their departure for Colombo. Just then, intelligence was received, by means of scouts, that the elephants, to the number of forty, were in full march towards the kraal. This set us all on the tip-toe of expectation. Every one betook himself to his appointed place. Ladies shrank away from the front seats, and I detected one or two of my own sex casting anxious glances towards the stairs. An equal bustle was visible within the kraal. The head Korale rushed about full of importance; the black stewards, with their white wands grouped themselves into parties of three or four, at irregular intervals amongst the jungle surrounding the open space, and especially about the entrance; but what duty was to be performed by these gentry, was more than I could divine. It is true (I was told by a native chief) that it would devolve on them to drive back any of the elephants, when caught in the kraal, in the event of their attempting to force the surrounding defences; but the idea of these poor creatures—some of them mere boys—being of any service, with their little white sticks, appeared so absurd and altogether ridiculous, that I thought I was being hoaxed by the Korale.

The shades of evening descended, and scouts continued to arrive from the driving party, with injunctions to hold everything in readiness, for the herd were coming on. The few torches that had been left to dispel the gloom were put out, or removed from sight. The moon had not risen. Every tongue was silent, save a few low whispers at intervals. Eyes were eagerly strained towards the opening through which the herd was expected to rush. Every ear was on the stretch to catch the most remote sounds in that direction. One might have fancied, from the death-like stillness of the place, that we were there awaiting our own fate, instead of that of elephants.

We did not wait long in this suspense. A distant shouting burst suddenly upon our startled ears. It drew rapidly nearer, and soon we could distinguish the violent cracking and snapping of branches of trees and low jungle. Then we heard the quick tramp of many ponderous and huge feet. There was no doubt but that the animals were close upon us; for torches were visible in the direction from which they were coming: indeed the distant jungle appeared to be alive with lights. Every native stood to his arms, such as they were. I could see the white wands glimmering about in the black forest at our feet: some score or two of rifle-barrels, long and ugly-looking instruments, of native make, were protruded from various points. Several of the ladies of our party wept; and I verily believe that some of the males wished inwardly that they were of the other sex, to have the privilege of fainting and being carried out of reach of danger. But there was little time for attention, even to frightened ladies. Our eyes were fixed upon the moving and rapidly approaching lights. They appeared to burn less brightly as they came nearer: then some disappeared, and soon the whole were extinguished, and all was plunged in darkness. Still, on came the furious monsters: bamboos crashed; the thick jungle flew about in splinters. A heavy tramping and tearing, and snapping asunder of branches,—and there they were, safely within the kraal. Then arose a shout, as the clouds and earth were about to meet, or to do something out of the common way. I bent forward to catch a peep at the enemy. The native body-guard waved their white wands. The entrance was barred up in a twinkling, and the torches brought forward to enable us to witness the proceedings, when a volley of loud uproarious laughter fell upon our ears, blended with exclamations of angry disappointment. All eyes were strained towards the clump of trees in the centre of the enclosure, where we beheld a dozen or two of flaming *chules* or torches, waved to and fro by some score of half-frantic villagers; and there, as the glare of torchlight burst through the dense gloom, we beheld crouching together, in place of forty huge elephants, a knot of village buffaloes, panting, and trembling, and tossing their heads. A survey of those creatures told us how the matter stood. There had been torches fastened to their horns, and one or two of them had the remains of *chules* hanging to their tails. There could not be a shadow of doubt that the affair had been a cruel hoax, and we were not long in ascribing the origin of it to the real perpetrators—the party of young coffee-planters with whom I had slept in the Padé boat.

The laughter of the evening, however, was not yet at an end. The light of innumerable *chules*, now moving about, discovered to us three nervous gentlemen snugly perched high among the branches of a tree close by our stand. They had made a rush up, in the first alarm of the onset; but, however easy fear had made the ascent, they evidently found it a somewhat difficult task to descend. All eyes were at once fixed upon the unlucky climbers, whose struggles to reach the lower branches were hailed with roars of furious laughter. Elephants, and buffaloes, and hoaxers were for the moment forgotten. One of them was the District Judge, a somewhat cumbruous personage; another, was an Assistant Agent, and the third, a Commissioner of the Court of Requests, a thin wiry fellow with a remarkably red face. There they were, kicking, and straining, and struggling in as pretty a fix as any of the Civil Service had ever found themselves; and it was not until some bamboos and ropes had been handed up to them, that they were able to reach the stand, and thence wend their way off the scene.

By the time the kraal was cleared, the night was far advanced, and the moon high in the horizon. Advice then reached us that the elephants had made a detour from the line, and had taken it into their unruly heads to treat themselves to a gambol across some score or two acres of prairie land; where they were amusing themselves with a good round game, despite the coaxing of a decoy consisting of two tame elephants. It was clear that nothing would be done on that night, and our merry parties betook themselves back to the village.

Our number were evidently on the decline next day. The patience of many had been exhausted. Towards evening intelligence was brought in, that thirty-five elephatnts, of all sizes, were in full march towards us; and, shortly afterwards, the Government Agent of the district, and the native chief of the Korle, came in from the driving, to see that all was made ready for the proper reception of the jungle visitors. Again all was hurry and bustle. Provision baskets and nervous ladies were sent to the rear: wine-bottles were placed in reserve, and sundry parting salutes were made with packets of sandwiches. Once more silence reigned over the kraal: torches were removed: the guards and watchers were doubled, and an extra supply of the little white wands brought to the front.

It was about two hours after dark when we heard the first distinct shouts of the drivers, who were slowly forcing the elephants towards the kraal; the two tame ones leading the way, and pointing out the advantages of that particular path to their jungle friends. Those sounds seemed to approach us at irregular intervals. Sometimes it appeared as though the animals were were not to be moved on any account, and the shouting died away; again they drew rapidly near; then paused; then forward, until we fancied we could distinguish the fall of the elephants' huge feet amongst the thick underwood. At last there was no mistake about it; they were close upon us. Our anxiety and curiosity became intense. The tearing and trampling amongst the jungle was deafening. Giant bamboos and branches of trees appeared to be snapped asunder by the on-coming herd, like so many walking-sticks—

in a way, in short, which made me tremble for the strength of the kraal, and of our own elevated platform.

But there was little time for reflection of any kind. A shot or two was fired in the rear of the advancing herd, followed by a trampling of the leading elephants. The moon at that moment began to peep over the distant range of low hills; and, by its faint light, I could distinguish the low jungle bending and giving way on every side, and amongst it sundry huge black forms rushing about in savage disorder, like mountain masses up-heaved by some convulsion of nature. The two decoys entered the enclosure at a brisk but steady trot, and stationed themselves under the clump of trees, without any notice being taken of them; indeed, one of them nodded knowingly to the Korale near him, as much as to say, "It's all right, old fellow!" On came the wild elephants at a thundering pace, tearing and bending, and smashing everything before them; trumpeting and roaring at full pitch. In another moment they were within the boundaries of our fortress.

Never shall I forget the wild, strange beauty of that uproarious moment. The moon was now shining sufficiently on the kraal to light up the more open parts of it; away under the deep shade on one side, could be seen a dense, moving mass of living creatures; huge, mis-shapen, and infuriated, trembling with rage and fatigue. Lighted *chules* were gleaming thickly, like fire-flies, amidst the neighbouring jungle. Felled trees and rope barred up the narrow way, forming one monster gate; whilst busy groups of villagers, white wands in hand moved to and fro, and watched the furious herd. More lights were brought to the front, and a blazing fire was kindled outside the entrance, which, whilst it served to light up the whole kraal, deterred the savage strangers from attempting anything in that direction.

It was soon evident that the prisoners were not going to take matters very quietly. Two of the stoutest of their number slowly advanced and examined the walls, to see where an opening might most easily be forced. And now we were not less astonished than delighted at the use made of those tiny white wands, which had before served only to raise our contempt. Wherever the two elephant spies approached the jungle-walls of their prison, they were met by one or two villagers, who gently waved before them little snow-white switches; and, lo! as if by some spell of potent forest magic, the beasts turned back, skrinking from contact with the little wands. Point after point was thus tried, but all in vain; the snowy magic sticks were thick within the jungle, and silently beat back the advancing foe.

While the two scouts were thus engaged on their exploring expedition, the tame elephants approached the remainder of the herd, and walked slowly round them, shaking their shaggy ears and waving high in air their curling trunks, as though they would say, "Move at your peril." One of the captives, a somewhat juvenile and unsophisticated elephant, ventured to move from the side of its maternal parent, to take a survey of our stand, when tame elephant Number One went up to the offender, and sent him back with an enormous flea in his ear; tame elephant number two bestowing at the same moment a smart tap on its skull.

Busier work was at hand. The scouts, evidently disgusted with the result of their operations upon the outworks, appeared to be preparing for a *sortie*, and treated with the most reckless levity the admonitory taps of the elephant policemen: which, however, seemed to be far less unpleasant to them than a tickle on the snout from one of the pigmy white wands. It was plain that they intended to carry their object by a *coup de trunk*; but a score of rifles peered forth. The ladies shut their eyes, and stopped their ears; an elderly gentleman, at my elbow, asked, in a tremulous whisper, "what the guns were for?" The inquiry was replied to by a loud trumpeting from one of the pair of rebels,—a harsh screaming roar, like the hollow sound of a strained railway whistle, very much out of repair. We had scarcely time to look at the poor brute creating this disturbance, when we heard the sharp crack of a dozen rifles around us—so sharp indeed, that our eyes blinked again. Down tumbled one of the monsters with thick torrents of hot, savage blood, pouring from many a wound about his head and neck. His companion was not so easily disposed of, though badly wounded. Lifting his enormous trunk in the air, and bellowing forth a scream of defiance, he made a rush at the jungle-wall. The two elephantine policemen who had been narrowly observing his proceedings, then made in between him and the ramparts, and succeeded in turning him from his purpose; but only to cause his to renew his fierce attack upon another part of the defences. He rushed at full speed upon the spot where our stand was erected, screaming and lashing his great trunk about him, as a schoolboy would a piece of whipcord. I felt alarmed. It seemed as though our frail tenement must yield at the first touch from the mighty on-coming mass of flesh, bone, and muscle. Ladies shrieked and fainted by the dozen: gentlemen scrambled over each other towards the stairs, where a decidedly downward tendency was exhibited. I would have given a trifle, just then, to have been where the day before were the Judge and the Collector, high amongst the branches. But in much less time than I take to relate it, the furious animal, smarting under many bullet wounds, had reached the verge of our stand, heedless of the cracking of rifles, whose leaden messengers flew round his head and poured down his shoulders, many harmless. One last crack and down the monster fell, close at our feet. That shot was the work of a mere lad, the little son of a Kandian Korale, who, coolly biding his time, had fired his piece close at the creature's ear. Leaping from his place, the urchin flung aside his long tapering rifle, and drawing forth his girdle-knife, servered the elephant's tail from the carcase, as his just trophy.

These two having been disposed of, and a degree of calm restored, the general attention was directed towards the herd, which still remained in their original position. For a time fear seemed to hold them motionless; but when the extremity of their danger rose before them, a number of the boldest made a desperate rush at the entrance, but were easily turned back when the watchers stirred up the great guard-fire, whilst, from other parts of the kraal, they were soon repelled by an application of white wands. In this way a good hour was spent, at the end of which time the creatures appeared to give up the idea of any further aggressive proceedings, and remained subdued and calm.

A dangerous task had still to be performed—that of securing the best of the herd for taming. Half-a-dozen of the most active and skilful of the villagers crept slowly and carefully towards the frightened group; each having a long stout cord of jungle-rope in his hand, with a running noose at one end of it. With stealthy, cat-like steps, these daring fellows went amongst the herd, making some of us tremble for their safety. Each of them selected one of the largest and strongest of the group, behind which they crept; and, having arranged the "lasso" for action, they applied a finger gently to the right heel of their beast, who feeling the touch as though that of some insect, slowly raised the leg, shook it, and replaced it on the ground. The men, as the legs were lifted, placed the running nooses beneath them, so that the elephants were quietly trapped, unknown to themselves, and with the utmost ease. They then slipped rapidly away with the ends of the ropes, and immediately made them fast to the trunks of the nearest trees. The ropes, however, were far from being sufficiently strong to hold an elephant who might put out his strength. It was therefore, necessary to secure them still further, but by gentle means. The two tame elephants were then placed on active service: they were evidently perfectly at home, and required no directions for their work. Walking slowly up to the nearest of the six captured animals, they began to urge him towards the tree to which he was fastened. At first the creature was stubborn; but a few taps on his great skull, and a mighty push on his carcase, sent him a yard or two nearer his destination. As he proceeded, the man in charge of the rope gathered in the slack of it; and so matters went on between this party—a tap, a push, and a pull—until at length three of the elephants were close to as many trees. Two other villagers then came forward with a stout iron chain. The tame animals placed themselves one on each side of a prisoner, pressing him between them so tightly as to prevent the possibility of his moving. In a minute or two the great chain was passed several times round the hind legs and the tree; and, in this way the captive was left; helpless and faint with struggling. The other five were similarly treated. After which our party dispersed, pretty well tired, and quite prepared for bed.

Early next morning I paid a last visit to the kraal, alone; my friends were fairly worn out. The remainder of the elephants had been either shot or had forced their way out in one or two places. The six captured animals were quiet—as well they might be, after their long fast and incessant struggling. Towards the end of that day, a very small portion of food was supplied to them, just sufficient to keep them alive. In this way they were to remain for a week or two, when, if found sufficiently reduced in strength and temper, they were to be walked about, fastened between two tame companions, who assisted very effectually in their daily education—not, perhaps, in the most gentle and polite manner, but still much to the purpose.

At the end of two or three months, the wild and unruly destroying monster of the jungle, might be seen quietly and submissively piling logs of timber in the Government yard, with a purpose-like intelligence little short of that of man.

A HAPPY VALLEY.

THERE was a spot not far from Lanka's latest capital, so rich in sylvan scenery, so favored by nature in soil and climate and locality, that they who knew its brightness, the sunny, cheerful life of those who dwelt there, called it "The Happy Valley."

The Vale of Dombera was not always what it is. There was a time, when, from one end to the other, the sweet aroma of the coffee blossom, blended with fragrance from the lime and orange flowers, loaded the air with perfume. One long undulating stretch of coffee gardens, from Rajahwella at one extremity, to Yahagaha Pitiya at the other, gave pleasant homes and busy occupations for a dozen Europeans whose well-kept bungalows were dotted through the valley. It was a good morning's ride from one end to the other; and in those days when coffee fields were interspersed with jungle and wild spots of low underwood and swampy ground, there was game to be found for the seeking,—game in abundance, large and small.

Kondesallie, with its sylvan homestead and its long undulating fields of coffee, was the parent of them all. About the Manager's pretty bungalow, there were signs of English care and thrift; a poultry yard with cows and pigs roaming about in happy indolence, gave to the place an air of comfort which was good to see. The plantation was threaded by many winding roads bordered by rose trees blossoming in one continuous round of never-ending summer.

To the north of this charming spot, was then to be seen the smaller but not less picturesque plantation of Gal Madua, equally undulating, equally rich in verdure and fertility, equally well roaded. Beyond it, was situated the little model estate of Talwatte, younger and smaller; and beyond that, again, further to the north, amidst broad acres of green patenas and pretty sylvan glades, and vallies and some topes of palms and arekas, was Yahagaha Pitiya, the bungalow of which stood on a green knoll from which no signs of coffee were visible, every planted field being hid by belts of jungle or groves of jak and bread-fruit trees. From this charming spot, this oasis amidst oases, the sweetest glimpses of scenery were to be had.

The huge rock at Matale, the lofty peak of Hunasgiria, the Knuckles range, the Medamahanuwera hills, and away to the west, the beetling crest of Hantane towering above many a hill and valley. Nearer, was to be seen a wide expanse of undulating grass land, threaded by strips of paddy fields, with

here and there a Headman's rustic dwelling, revelling amidst a thick grove of palms and jaks. For many a long mile, the wide expanse of verdure lay stretched like a carpet, until, in the distance, woodland and dells and undulating hills were blended in one broad green landscape.

At one extremity of this "Happy Valley" the path led to a pretty grassy walk overshaded by massive wide spreading banyan and other trees, through the long vista of whose pleasant foliage an ancient Dagoba was visible far in the distance, besides which stood a "Pansela" in which an old priest had dwelt for a life-time: from Yahagaha Pitiya to this pretty sylvan spot, was a favorite evening stroll, and there, the planter and his family often sauntered; and seated at the old man's porch, held converse with him on subjects upon which he loved to speak—the past history of his country, the heroic deeds of a long race of sovereigns passed away.

On the south side of the Valley, were, adjoining Kondesallie, the thriving, picturesque estate of Pallikelle, partly of coffee, partly sugar, and the Deegalle Coffee plantation, and beyond that the fine property of Rajahwella, whose rich, deep, loamy soil and excellent situation, marked it out for a long and prosperous career. Between these various properties, were open grass lands, patenas, on which the estate cattle found abundant pasturage, and across which the Managers were able to enjoy a good morning canter, when work fell slack, which it did not often; for in those early days labor was far less plentiful than at present: the few Tamils obtainable, had to be supplemented by Kandyan villagers, a most fickle and uncertain class of workmen, with an occasional draft of low country Singhalese, a still more unstable element in the planter's calculation of work to be done.

Nowhere in all Ceylon was there at that time such a wide stretch of Coffee as in the Vale of Dumbera. The mountains and vallies of the Kandyan country were then one vast mass of forest, untouched by planter's axe, save here and there a small solitary clearing, the nurseries of a future gigantic industry. On the Hantane and Hunasgeria ranges, away upon the Knuckles, in the Kallibokke valley, and anon in Pusilava, gaps had been made in the dense jungle, but few and far between. Seen from above, these pioneer clearings would appear like specks on the wide ocean of forest below, with here and there at long intervals, a small curling wreath of smoke rising from the planter's solitary hut of mud and talipot. Not a mile of roadway was to be seen throughout that great stretch of forest; not a bridge spanned any river; all save our "Happy Valley" was a vast expanse of jungle solitude, the silence of which was only broken by the roar of the elephant, the tread of the buffalo, or the cry of some winged dweller in the woods, disturbed by village sportsmen. Travellers and holiday-makers from the central capital, were in those days, attracted by the novelty of Coffee estates in full vigor, to drive to the Kondesallie ferry, stroll over the cultivated fields, look in at the sugar works, call on the Manager, and drive back to Kandy, convinced that they had beheld the germ of what was one day in the remote future, to become a marvellously expanded and wealth-bestowing enterprise. It has realised all these expectations to the full; but alas at the cost of how many lives, how many shattered fortunes and broken constitutions!

Then, all was bright, sunny hopefulness. Seasons and markets were less unstable than they have since been found: the virgin soil was full of undeveloped vigor, and yielded readily abundant crops, without a thought of fertilising agents. If salaries were in those days small, they were at least ample for the planters' wants; when full grown fowls were three pence each, eggs two shillings a hundred; and as for beef, you could have the shooting of a buffalo on any foggy morning, when cattle trespassers found their forbidden way amongst the young fields of Pallikelle sugar cane.

It was not all sunshine in that fertile valley: there was a price to be paid for the wonderful abundance of the crops, that season after season were gathered on the Dumbera plantations. If the soil were fertile, it was rank with noxious exhalations: but recently opened by the axe, the plough or the mamotie, it was found that what favored vegetable life, was fatal to animal health. In those portions of the valley which bordered on the steamy banks of the Mahavilla ganga, fever asserted full sway, and carried off its victims by the score. So terrible was its effects, that on some occasions all field work came to a dead lock; every available cooly on the Deegalle estate was fully occupied in attending to the sick or burying the dead. The Europeans did not escape. Superintendents were invalided rapidly, and the Manager, a well known planter of iron constitution and of marvellous spirits, was the only person on the estate who was not prostrated by the scourge. In the end, disease swept away the whole available force of coolies on the estate, and it became a very serious question as to how the growing crop of Coffee was to be gathered and cured. Coolies must be had; but where, was the question. The estate was so notorious in Kandy and its neighbourhood for unhealthiness, that it was in vain to hope for recruits in that direction. A fine piece of finesse was resorted to, in order to seduce unsuspecting Tamils to the locality. To have sent one of the superintendents stricken with fever, as they were, to enlist coolies, would have been as futile as to have mentioned the name of the estate for which their services were required: a wiser plan was carried into successful execution. The services of a young, ruddy-faced planter, from one of the adjacent estates were secured, and he was despatched with a fair supply of rupees and a couple of burly canganies, not to Kandy, but to Matale on the north road, the halting-place of immigrant coolies, on their way from the coast of India. There a few scores of them were engaged by the healthy-looking planter, marched in safe custody by a circuitous route to the vale of Dumbera, and there handed over to the care of the Deegalle superintendent, who with sunken cheeks and hollow eyes mustered them on the barbacue and commenced by administering a strong dose of quinine to them all round. Before a month was spent the lives of half their number were as good as forfeited, and the rest were sore smitten with a mortal fear.

But though disease played havoc with some portions of this happy valley, it was upon the whole a cheerful, pleasant spot and something more, for it was oftentimes the scene of much boisterous roystering mirth. Tradition has told many a tale of noisy gatherings on Saturday evenings, of Knuckles' Bricks and Dumbera boys in Deegalle bungalow. How the revels were kept up until far into Monday morning, when steeds were saddled in hot haste, and many an aching head throbbed hotly as the muster-ground was reached at day-light.

The small bungalow in which these protracted revels were held, has long since disappeared: its site thickly overgrown with thorny brushwood and lantana, was once sought for by friends of one of the early planters and was at length discovered by the vast memorial mound of empty bottles piled up about the lonely spot.

The daring spirits of those early time who sometimes gave too much to the rosy god, and wasted in revelry the energies that were often overtaxed in heavy continuous work, amidst privations unknown to planters of to-day, rarely if ever trenched on the proper hours of work, but gave without stint to their employers every hour of thought and toil that conld be claimed. But hardy as were these planting pioneers, they were but mortal: there were limits to their endurance, and those bounds too often reached, claimed, though late, all the penalties that disregarded laws of nature could exact.

Times have changed since then, and so have places. Years have rolled onwards remorselessly, blighting many a fond hope. A panic time of trouble and dismay brought desolation to the valley once so happy. Beggared proprietors and bankrupt agents sought aid in vain from penniless bankers, and in the end well cared for estates with bungalows, and works and coolies' lines were sold for less than the land once cost. Money seemed to have fled the country, and so men grew callous and let the bramble usurp the place of coffee, and the relentless lanthana claim for its own the fairest fields in that fair valley. The buffalo trampled down the honeysuckle and the vine, the wild boar made his home amidst the roses: and where the prattling sounds of tiny voices were once heard, the jackall shrieked at night-fall.

Once more a change has come over this bright vale of sunshine: once more the cheerful sounds of pleasant voices are heard o'er many an acre, and once again human industry asserts its supremacy over the jungle. One large hearted toiler has made his home down there, and by the sheer force of skilful labor has rescued the land from barrenness, and made it what it was in olden, long-forgotten times, a "Happy Valley."

OUR PRODUCE DEALER.

TEN miles an hour,—not a yard less, dashing through horse-traps and water gullies in the road, over treacherous heaps of broken metal, along the edges of dangerous drains, skirting ugly-looking culverts, on goes that fast-trotting mare, black as night, sleek as velvet, safe as anything, through Panadura, dashing into Morotuwa, scaring hackery bullocks, scattering groups of children at Ratmalane, and flying like a puff of dark wind past sober hired horses along Colpetty. The whip is a middle aged Singhalese, clad in purest white, with showy gold buttons on his jacket, watch and chain, and the tallest of marvellous combs in his hair. He is a dealer in produce generally, but in two articles especially. Matthes Appoo was in early life much attached to coir, and in pursuing the bent of his affection in the direction of that especial article, he had become an adept. He knew to a nicety, how much jackwood dye badly colored yarn would stand, without betraying the hand of the manipulator, and had made money by the device. But yarn was slow work, and he eventually abandoned his first love for two other more attractive, because more remunerative objects,—cinnamon and plumbago. There is no sort of similarity in these two, on the contrary—one is very heavy, the other is very light—one is dug from the bowels of the earth, the other is shaved off, if we may so say, from the earth's surface. There is this, however, in common between them, they are both valuable articles, and are both susceptible of a good deal of manipulation, so much so indeed, that they might almost be classed as art-manufactures, instead of as raw-products, seeing how much "cooking" enters into their composition.

Matthes began his commercial and manufacturing career, at an early age : he had served his time to an uncle, and under him had acquired a knowledge of many little matters, which were afterwards turned to profitable account on a larger scale : at fourteen he had become an adept at bargaining for cinnamon, sorting it and even at "making it up," which is the technical or artistic term for blending the bark of the real cinnamon plant, with that of spurious spice, or of trees which have no relationship to the "laurus" family. There is an active trade carried on in America in wooden nutmegs. Ceylon can equally boast its guava cinnamon, and its "laterite" plumbago.

Beholding the dashing "whip" of the Galle road, one would scarcely imagine the humbleness of his first beginnings in the outskirt of Maradana: beneath the shady roof of a primitive hovel, and a ricketty out-house, rented at eight shillings a month, he mapped out his future career, content to bide his time with small beginnings, his cheap and simple conveyance at that period of his life was a bullock-hackery. His first essays in the dying of worthless coir yarn, yielded him profit, and gave him the means to lay in a stock of "palm oil," which he distributed with great tact, amongst the storekeepers and head coolies, of the principal exporters in the Fort.

It was a saying of a former popular Governor of Ceylon, that "the best lubricator for the wheels of the State, is champagne :" the State wheels ran pleasantly enough in his time. Matthes was of pretty much the same opinion in regard to the wheels of fortune, sparing neither thirty shilling champagne, nor two-guinea brandy with gilt labels. Those who spend but little on themselves, can afford to be liberal to others, especially when sprats are given to catch herrings, and even larger fish. No wonder then, that the little shady hovel, and its ricketty godowns in the black slums of Maradana, were soon exchanged for a tiled dwelling, and a range of solid godowns, at we are afraid to guess how much monthly rent, in one of the main thoroughfares, at a convenient distance from water carriage, and not very remote from the family abodes of the storekeepers of two large buyers of native produce. Cheerful, and occasionally not unprofitable evenings, were spent in the society of the said storekeepers, who sipped Matthes's liquor in the front verandah, and chatted about coir, cinnamon, and plumbago, in the most satisfactory manner, until it was hard to say which were more sold, the produce or the masters.

But no matter how many corks were drawn on these occasions, the dealer was up at the usual hour to take his early bath, and seek for the early worm, which he generally managed to find. Coffee and hoppers despatched, his people began to arrive, and by seven o'clock operations were in full play. There were the cinnamon storing rooms, the coir steeping rooms, and beyond all, in later days, in another compound, the plumbago manufactory, in which cart loads of "laterite," or vulgarly "cabook," were converted into the finest plumbago, by the skilled myrmidons of this 'Wizard of the East.' Within his long range of godowns, there were many chambers with intricate divisions and entrances, all piled with produce in various stages of manipulation, and we may as well add in varied modes, to suit the different tastes or capacities of the dealer's buyers. For the lately landed British merchant, fresh and green from the environs of Cornhill, Matthes had bales of the smoothest and most golden looking spice that ever Spanish Don set eyes upon: these were the produce of an extensive tract of young guava trees in Saffragam, peeled, prepared and dried as cinnanmon, and so closely resembling it in general appearance, save that it was too pale and too smooth, that unwary buyers might easily be imposed upon by it; but what about the sweet odour and the still sweeter-taste peculiar to the bark of cinnamon: this is managed in a few hours by immersion in large tubs of the waste water from the distillation of cinnamon oil, and afterwards when dry, by the slightest touch on each end of a bundle of the false guava pipes, with a cloth saturated with cheap cinnamon oil, which leaves behind it a searching and tolerably permanent aroma. this perfume, and the taste left by cinnamon water, are quite sufficient for the newly caught shipper of native produce, eager as he is to develop the resources of the country and add to his own. For the buyer who has been two or three years in the country, and has had an awakening to a sense of the existence of guava trees* in Ceylon, our dealer has other varieties of spice, almost as worthless, but less easy of detection: these are the produce of spurious varieties of the cinnamon plant, grown in the jungles of the interior, and when cut young, presenting a good deal of the external appearance of the genuine article: this too is doctored in the manner prescribed, and as eagerly bought by the advanced griffin. A third mode of manipulation is by false packing, which consists in filling the centres of pipes of good cinnamon with pieces of guava bark or of spurious cinnamon: this requires skilful operation and when well worked is not easily detected. The sale of guava or jungle bark, which probably costs about six pence the pound in Colombo, in place of spice worth from eighteen pence to two shillings in ordinary years, must be a lucrative business if a dealer can transact much of it, and that much of it does change hands at these prices, advices from home assure us, equally with the increasing wealth of Matthes and his co-traders.

The plumbago trade has grown up marvellously of late: from small beginnings it has come to be, like our friend Matthes amongst shippers, in great request. Its value has doubled, and its exports have trebled in not very many years.

---

* In Mincing Lane this guava spice is termed sassafrass bark, though why is difficult to understand, as the sassafrass tree is totally different in growth and quality from the guava tree.

In former times it was known chiefly as a lubricant, and a polishing powder for fire grates, and some other such purposes. Now its chief use is in the construction of crucibles for melting obstinate metals, and again for a very different purpose, in the manufacture of pencils in substitution of Cumberland lead which is becoming more scarce and dearer year by year. For both these latter purposes it is essential that the article be pure and free from sand or soil of any kind, and in proportion to this quality is its value. A shipper who is careful on this point will insist on seeing every barrel filled and packed in his own yard, before paying for it, yet with all this precaution, he is not unfrequently sold by a clever legerdemain between storekeepers and dealers, who occasionally manage to pack away some of the cabook covered by plumbago artfully rubbed over it. Some wholesale frauds of this kind have been known to take place, always of course, with connivance on the part of some subordinate in the shipper's employ. The most notable instance of the kind occurred some dozen years ago, when a loss of nearly a thousand pounds, was sustained by a large exporter of plumbago who had most carefully seen to the filling, packing and marking of every barrel of the finest plumbago. Our friend the clever manipulator of guava cinnamon, was in this case equal to the occasion. He had supplied the fine silvery mineral and the barrels, and his men had assisted in marking the packages for the merchant. His procedure was to fill a like number of similar barrels with rubbishing plumbago dust, mark the packages with the same numbers and marks which are usually very simple, generally one or at most two letters, send his barrels to the wharf on the same day with the others, and then for a dextrous quick hand to go carefully round in the dead of the night, and by the light of a dark-lanthorn, mark a cross or a star below the distinguishing letter on all the barrels of good plumbago. On the morrow when the coolies went to load the plumbago in boats, they naturally loaded the barrels containing the rubbish as they alone had the mark indicated in the shipping order, the others with the star beneath the initial letter, they of course left on the wharf, and these were afterwards either removed to the dealer's premises, or sold as they stood on the wharf ready for shipment, and being found of first rate quality, fetched a high price. It is scarcely necessary to add that the shipper who had such a long and angry correspondence with his American constituents, to whom he made the consignment, never succeeded in tracing the manner of the fraud or the perpetrators.

But let it not be supposed that all produce dealers are as Matthes Appoo, given to manipulations of a doubtful kind. It is not so. We do not care to venture on any guesses as to the proportion which manipulating dealers bear to the plain and straight-forward dealing contractors who conscientously give you the article they profess to sell; suffice it to say there are somewhat too many of the former to make the life of a young beginner at merchandising, quite one of velvet and roses. That they are thus numerous is matter for deep regret. But on the other hand, there are dealers, Singhalese and Tamil, whose word may be taken as their bond, and whose goods will pass the most cunning scrutiny without fail or fault. Meantime Matthes has married the dowered daughter of a wealthy cart-contractor, and has taken a suburban villa somewhere in the direction of Mount Lavinia so as to be handy for the plumbago business. He has a number of pits giving employment to some scores of workpeople, who bring to the surface many tons of the mineral monthly. At first Matthes had no idea, but that of getting a few facilities from the headmen in the matter of royalty, but when his pada-boats were delayed, sometimes for weeks together, for the Mudeliyar to come and see to the weighing of the plumbago, he became so exasperated that it needed small persuasion to induce him to despatch his boat loads of the mineral, without the operation of weighing, or the formality of paying the royalty; and none were the wiser. That which he adopted at first in self-defence, he now practices from force of habit, and as he keeps a store of good liquor always at hand, the overworked headman does not trouble himself to enquire whether the amount of royalty paid by Matthes can possibly represent the extent of business he must do, to build up the fortune he is evidently making.

NUMBER FORTY-TWO.

THE true, original Number Forty-two—of which a copy may be seen in any of the thousands of towns and cities between Nepaul and Ceylon—is situated in the very heart of the black town of Colombo, amidst the streets in which dwell natives, half-castes, and Eurasians, or country-born descendants of Europeans: it is to be found in the chief thoroughfare of the town, if such a term as thoroughfare can properly be applied to the narrow, choked-up street, boiling over with hot coolies, and enraged bullock-drivers.

This state of tropical conglomeration will be more readily understood when I mention that the carriage-way or street is the only passage available for pedestrians and equestrians, for bipeds and quadrupeds. The Dutch, when masters of the place, had provided every house with broad luxuriant verandahs, covered in and nicely paved; so that the dwellers in the town might not only sit out under shade in the open air at eventide; but, during the furious heat of the day, could walk from one end of the street to the other under these broad and pleasant covered ways. Now,* many of these verandahs have been appropriated and railed off, as open receptacles of all sorts of merchandise. Where in former jolly days, radiant Dutchmen sat and smoked their pipes, and quaffed Schiedam, are now piled up motley goods to tempt the unwary passer-by. Where buxom, merry-eyed lasses once flirted with incipient burgomasters, are shiploads of rice, and cargoes of curry stuffs. The perfume of the rose and the oleander are supplanted by the caustic fragrance of garlic and salt-fish.

---

* A. D. 1848.

Dotted along this fragrant street, among rice stores, iron depôts, and dried fish warehouses, are the shops of the Moormen traders, the only attractions for Europeans in this quarter. Your regular Moorman shopkeepers, or bazaar-men, possess such terrifically unpronounceable names that, by common consent, their English customers designate them by the numbers of their shops. In this way a little, thin-faced, shrivelled-up Moorman, a small portion of whose name consists of Meera Lebbe Slema Lebbe Tamby Ahamadoe Lebbe Marcair, is cut down to Number Forty-eight; which is the title he is known by.

The most flourishing of these gentry is certainly Number Forty-two; a portly, oily-skinned, well-conducted Moorman, with a remarkably well-shaved head, surmounted on its very apex by a ridiculously little colored cap, like an infantine bee-hive. His bazaar is admitted on all hands, especially amongst the fair sex, to be "first chop." Yet a stranger would imagine that the fiscal had possession of the place and was on the point of selling off by auction the entire contents: so confused and motley an appearance do they wear.

The doorway, narrow and low, is jealously guarded by a pile of grindstones, surmounted by a brace of soup-tureens on the one side, and by tools and weapons of offence on the other; so that the chances are that, in trying to escape the Newcastle and Staffordshire Charybdis you get caught upon the sharp points of the Sheffield Scylla. Once past these dangers, however, you forget all your anxiety and nervousness in the bland sunny countenance of Numbr Forty-two. He is truly delighted to see you, he is so anxious to place the whole contents of his store at your complete dísposal, that one might fancy his sole object in life was to minister to the pleasure of the English community.

Number Forty-two directs your attention, in the most winning manner, to a choice and very dusky collection of hanging lamps of the most grotesque fashion. His fowling-pieces are pointed out to you as perfect marvels. If you require any blacking-brushes, or padlocks, or Windsor soap, or smoking caps, or tea-kettles, he possesses them in every possible variety, just out by the very latest ship.

Our bazaar is by no means aristocratic. On the contrary, it is most decidedly republican in all its tendencies. It admits of no distinction of ranks. The highest born wares are placed on an equal footing with the most lowly merchandise, the most plebeian goods. Earthenware jostles cut-glass; ironmongery—and some of it rare and rusty too—elbows the richest porcelain; vulgar tin-ware hob-nobs with silks and satins. Tart-fruits and pickles revel in the arms of forty yards of the best crimson velvet. Pickled salmon in tins are enshrined amongst Coventry ribbons.

I don't happen to require any of his perfumery or preserves, nor am I anxious about muslins or plated-candle-sticks: I simply want to select a few very plain wine-glasses, and I know there are none better than at Number Forty-two. Piles after piles of the fragile glass-ware are raked out from under a mass of agricultural implements, and it is really marvellous to see how harmlessly the brittle things are towsled and tumbled about amongst ponderous wares and massive goods. How peacefully the lions and the lambs of manufactures repose together within the dusty dark walls of Forty-two.

My friend with the bee-hive cap is never disconcerted by any demand, however out of the common way. From ships' anchors and chain-cables down to small minnikin-pins, he has a supply of every possible variety of wares. I have often asked for things that I never dreamt of requiring, just to try the wonderful resources of Number Forty-two, and sure enough he would produce the articles one by one. I thought I had caught him once when I requested to look at a few warming-pans, and pictured to myself how hugely chap-fallen he would appear, to be obliged to confess that he had no such things in his store. But not a bit of it. He stole away very placidly into some dismal dark hole of a place, amongst a whole cavern of bottles and jars, and just as I pictured him emerging into broad daylight, dead-beaten, he came npon me radiant and cheerful as ever, bearing a gigantic and genuine "warming-pan," apologising to me, as he removed the coating of dust from it, for having but that one to offer—it was the last of his stock.

There was one peculiarity about my friend with the bee-hive, which must not be omitted. He never made any abatement in the price demanded for his articles, be they of the latest importation, or the remains of an invoice standing over since he first started in business. A shop-keeper in nearly any other country in the world would, at the end of a certain number of years, clear out his old stock, and dispose of it as he best could, to make room for new wares. But not so Number Forty-two; nor indeed any other number in that bazaar. There lay the old-fashioned cotton-prints, and silk waistcoat pieces, and queer-looking ribbons of no colour at all. Years have rolled past since they first entered their present abode. The merchant who imported them died of a liver attack a dozen years since. They would not sell in eighteen hundred and thirty, and therefore are not very likely to move off in eighteen hundred and forty-eight; but the same price is affixed to them now as then, and the only chance for their disposal would seem to be by the direct interposition of a fire or an earthquake. Number Forty-two had doubtless heard that wines are improved by age, and he may possibly imagine that some mellowing and enriching process goes on in a lapse of years, with regard to silks and muslins.

This class of Indian shopkeepers have, moreover, a very confused and mystified conception of the real value of some goods. They can tell you to a trifle the worth of a dinner-set, or of a dozen of Dutch hoes, but in millinery and other fancy articles, they are often fearfully mistaken. A Moorman buys what is termed in technical language, a "Chow-chow" invoice, in other words, a mixed assortment of hardware and software, of workables and wearables. He is told the lot is valued at a hundred pounds sterling; he offers eighty, and takes them at ninety. He refers to the invoice on opening out the goods, and gets on very well in pricing them until he comes to such things as ribbons, gloves, lace, &c.; which are the dear and which the cheap he cannot possibly tell, and he therefore, tickets them at so much the yard or the pair all round, as the case may be. In this way I often pick up a glorious bargain at Forty-two, buying kid-gloves for eighteen-pence, for which in London I should have to pay at least four shillings; and a trifle of real Brussels lace for my wife, at the price of the very commonest Nottingham article.

The fortunes of Forty-two were once placed in the most imminent jeopardy from a circumstance which happened in his shop while I was there, and which became, at the time, the food of all the hungry gossip-mongers of the place. My friend had a Moorish assistant remarkably active, but dissipated and impertinent. He was ugly beyond measure, and when he grinned, which he frequently would do in spite of strict injunctions to the contrary, he distended a cavern of a mouth that was perfectly hideous. This creature had one day become unusually excited, and it appears in the fervour of his jollity had laid a wager with a young neighbour of kindred habits, that he would kiss the first female customer who should set foot within his master's shop on that morning, be she fair or dark. I can imagine the horror with which poor Forty-two beheld his grinning deputy fulfil his engagement by saluting the fair cheek of an English lady, and that lady—as chance would have it—the wife of one of the high legal functionaries of the place. The affair was hushed up as much as it could be, but in the end it oozed out; and people, so far from deserting Number Forty-two, actually flocked to it to hear the particulars of the affair. The offender was dismissed; but not until he had imparted to that particular shop an unenviable celebrity that might have ruined its owner.

There are other numbers besides Forty-two, which enjoy a considerable reputation, all things considered, but they certainly lack the fashionable repute of the aforesaid. For instance, there is Number Forty-seven, a remarkably well-conducted man, very steady, very civil, and exceedingly punctual in settling his accounts with the merchants who esteem him accordingly. This worthy Moorman transacts business much on the same principle as his neighbours, but unlike Forty two and one or two other active numbers, he is given to indulge in certain *siestas* during the heat of the day, which no influx of customers can debar him from enjoying. As the hour of high noon approaches, he spreads his variegated mat upon the little, dirty, ricketty, queer-looking couch, under the banana tree in the back court-yard by the side of the well, and there, under the pleasant leafy shade, he dozes off, fanned by such traunt breezes as have the courage to venture within such a cooped-up, shut-in pit of a yard, dreaming of customers, accounts and promisssory notes. During this slumber, it is in vain for any one to attempt to coax a yard of muslin, or a fish-kettle out of the inexorable Forty-seven. The somniferous spell has descended upon his dwarfy deputy, who, rather than wake his master, would forfeit his chance of Paradise; and he, no less drowsy himself, opens one eye and his mouth only, to assure you that the article you require is not to be found in their shop. You insist that it is. You know where to lay your hand upon it. The deputy Forty-seven shakes his drowsy head in somniferous unbelief. You seek it out from its dusty, murky hiding-place, and produce it before his unwilling face.

He opens another eye, smiles, nods to you, and is away again far into the seventh heaven. There is no help for it, but to appropriate the article and pay for it on your next visit.

Number Forty-eight is a small bustling variety of Moorman, making a vast show of doing a large stroke of business; but, as far as I could ever perceive, doing next to nothing. He bought largely, paid as regularly as most of other numbers, was constantly opening huge packing cases and crates, and sorting out their contents into heaps; but I never remembered to have seen a single customer within his shop. How the man lived was, for a long time, a perfect mystery to me; but I learnt at length that he disposed of his purchases entirely by means of itinerant hawkers who armed with a yard-measure and a pair of scales, and followed by a pack of loaded coolies groaning under huge tin cases and buffalo-skin trunks, perambulated from town to village, from house to hut; and by dint of wheedling, puffing, and flattering, succeeded in returning with a bag full of coin.

For Number Sixty-two I entertained a more than ordinary respect. Unlike his Moorish brethern he possessed a remarkably rational name,—Saybo Dora. Originally a hawker, he had by his steady conduct won the confidence of the merchants, who supplied him with goods wherewith to open a store, at a time when such places did not exist in the town. From small beginnings he rose to great transactions; and now, beside a flourishing trade in the bazaar, carried on pretty extensive operations in many smaller towns throughout the country. It was by no means an unusual thing for this simply-clad mean-looking trader to purchase in one day from one merchant, muslins to the value of a thousand pounds, crockery for half that amount, and perhaps, glassware for as much more. For these he would pay down one-fourth in hard cash, and so great was the confidence reposed in him, that his bags of rupees, labelled and endorsed with his name and the amount of their contents, were received and placed in the strong-room of the Englishman without being counted. Saybo Dora's name on the packages gave them currency.

So much for their business aspect; but once I paid a visit to Forty-two in his private dwelling. In one of the dullest, dirtiest, and most squalid-looking streets of the black town dwelt he of the bee-hive and portly person. The hut was perched high up on a natural parapet of red iron-stone, with a glacier of rubbish in front. The day had been fearfully hot, even for India; the very roadway was scorching to the feet though the sun had set, yet the tiny windows and the ramshackling doors were all closed. Nobody was lying dead in the house, as I first imagined might be the case. They had only shut out the heat.

I found Forty-two enveloped in a sort of winding-sheet, reclining on some coarse matting, and smoking a very large and dirty hookah. A brazen vessel was by his side, a brass lamp swung from the ceiling; and, on a curiously carved ebony stand, was a little sort of stew-pan minus a handle filled with sweet-meats. In an adjoining part of the dwelling, divided off only by some loose drapery for want of a door, lay sprawling on the earthen floor a leash of infantine, embryo Forty-twos; while, shrouded in an impenetrable mass of muslin, crouched Mrs. Forty-two, masticating tobacco leaves and betel nut. Smoking, eating sweatmeats and curry, and sleeping form the sum total of the earthly enjoyments of this race of people. Their sole exception to this dreary, caged existence being an occasional religious festival, or a pilgrimage to some shrine of great sanctity, when the muslin-shrouded wife, the muslin-less children, the sweetmeats, the hookah and the brazen vessels are packed into a hackery which, with its huge white bullock, jingles and creaks over the ruts and stones as though the wheels and axle had got a touch of Saint Vitus's dance, and for that one day, at any rate, Number Forty-two may be fairly said to be out of town.

OUR COFFEE MILLS.

THE fine old English gentleman, who sits at home at ease, and sips his morning coffee, with the *Times* upon his knees, is utterly powerless to fathom the depth of human ingenuity, which, during the last quarter of a century have been brought into the service of the coffee grower and the coffee curer. The frugal house-wife may marvel at the rapid strides with which the Ceylon article has risen in public estimation and general value at home and abroad, until it has nearly attained the foremost place amongst the coffees of the world.

The race for place between the coffee-producing countries of the world, has been a long and a waiting race, so far as Ceylon was concerned. She knew that the Mocha staple was a strong opponent, while the Jamaica and Costa Rica confederacies had long been favorites in the field, and could always command the odds: she did not care much for Brazils, and as for Java she was not fit for any distance. Well, for years past, Mocha has had all the running at heavy odds, say 100 to 85, with Jamaica a good second at 90 to 60, and Costa Rica well on her quarter at 85 to 65, Ceylon all the while waiting steadily upon them at 70 to 50, with Rio and Java in the crowd. But, places have been changed lately: there was some very close running in 1861, and now we find the Ceylon berry has regularly overhauled the Jamaica favorite and the Costa Rica pet, and left them behind, and is making capital running for first place. We shall expect to hear in the next report, that the Ceylon filly has won cleverly by a neck, with Jamaica and Costa Rica completely distanced.

How all this has happened does not take long to tell, so we will tell it and pass on to explain the means and appliances now in use throughout this city, for maintaining the high position its chief produce has attained. The cultivation of coffee in Ceylon has been all along, carried on under many disadvantages and drawbacks. Fickleness of seasons, instability of markets, uncertainty of labor supply, dearness and scarcity of transport, and, after all, a long voyage to market. To meet so many drawbacks our planters set themselves to see how they could lessen the cost of production and curing, and enhance the value of their product by greater care in the preparation. The latter object has led by slow degrees, to such improvements in machinery, processes, and appliance that coffee-curing has become a scientific process, and hence the presence of so many extensive buildings and tall chimneys which are to be seen in every direction in the neighbourhood of Colombo.

Forty years ago when coffee-curing was in its earliest stages of infancy, such a thing as a Coffee mill did not exist. The whole of the then small crops were dried on mats spread in the front and back yards of Colombo fort offices: not a bean of it was dried out of the fort, and the peeling or removal of the parchment covering of the berry was effected either by hand-peelers of a very rude and cumbrous make, or by peelers worked off the engines of two oil mills. It was, if we remember rightly, in the year 1840 that the first regular coffee-curing establishment was formed out of the fort, on the actual site of the present extensive Ambewelle mills, where may still be seen a small portion of the original old walls and doorways: well do we remember when the foundations of that unpretending coffee-curing store were laid, how British merchants came out to look at them, and shaking their sceptical heads, pronounced the firm which was engaged in the building, no better than insane, for that all the estates in Ceylon could never grow coffee enough to cover those vast brick barbacues; and as for the peeler-wheels shod with iron, why of course, they would crush all the coffee into triage! Such were the predictions of the Colombo magnates of 1840. We have lived to see thirty coffee mills each of ten times the capacity of the original coffee mill in Slave Island, and all find ample work, whilst the weight and speed of the "peeler" wheels have been doubled.

An account of the processes carried on in any one of these many mills will represent the work of the whole, for although the special arrangements and disposition of drying ground, peeling-house and picking and packing stores, may differ in certain details, they all follow one general principle.

A stranger to Ceylon and unacquainted with the vicissitudes of our climate, and the condition in which much of the first parcels of coffee are received from the estates, might well marvel at the massive character of the buildings, and the very finished manner in which every appliance is completed. We may as well inform those who are unacquainted with the fact, that in the early months of the coffee season, say from October to far into December, the weather is most variable, and the parchment coffee received from the planters, is often saturated with moisture to such an extent as to require a full week of good Colombo sunshine to free it of superfluous water, to say nothing of drying it for the mill. Of course, this makes the curing rather costly, and the freight by railway very high, as the charge for carriage is by weight. But it is often unavoidable from long-continued rains up-country, combined with a rush of ripe cherry blocking up the planters' stores, so as to prevent them from turning it over, and therefore rather than run the risk of heating, they consent to extra freight by railway and extra growls from the Colombo curers.

During October and November, the manager of a coffee mill leads a most harrassing life; anxious to take advantage of every blink of sunshine to air and if possibly, warm his wet parchment, he is compelled to run risks and cover his wide barbacues, as thinly as may be, and perhaps before it has had an hour of fresh, warm, morning air upon it, a heavy squall sweeps over the ground, and ere three-fourths of the damp coffee can be gathered up, and placed within shelter, the barbacues are swimming from the effects of the watery downpour.

When coffee is received from the estate, unless the season be far advanced, and there be hot dry weather up-country, the bean inside the parchment is usually so soft as to yield to pressure: as it would be impossible to remove the parchment from it in this condition, and as the soft coffee berry could not be preserved with so much water in its composition, it has to undergo a good deal of exposure to the sun.

It is not necessary in describing the process of coffee curing and packing, as carried on in Colombo, that we should give a sketch of any particular establishment. The mode of procedure is identical in all of them, though there may be modifications of arrangements in some not to be found in others, and some of the larger or more recently erected mills, have mechanical appliances for economising labor, not to be found in others. Apart from these arrangements, however, there is no essential difference in any of them.

Whether you enter the Blooming-hall Mills, or the United Channel Island Stores, or the New Banff establishment, between six and seven o'clock in the morning, the sight which meets your eye is pretty much the same. The female part of the indigenous population, will be streaming in to perform their daily task of coffee-picking, some Singhalese, some Tamil, some with sleeping babies or toddling children, some free from incumbrances, and thinking only of their new comboy of the richest magenta, and their gorgeous hair-pin, receiving the gate-keeper's knowing wink of the left eye, as an understood and legitimate tribute to their personal attractions. And here we may mention that in the coffee-picking world, fully as much as in the western, civilised world, "kissing goes by favor," and it is quite pleasant to see how readily the store coolies lighten the labors of a pretty and unencumbered picker;"

her allowance of coffee for the day's work is brought to the precise spot, close to an open breezy window where she works, her mat will be spread for her, and one might almost imagine though it would no doubt be a gross libel on the male portion of the establishment, that the bushel which measured her bag of coffee could not have been nearly so large as that which meted out the daily allowance of her neigbour, the haggard-looking woman with a squalling child.

Whilst these ladies are strolling in and assuming their alloted tasks, a score or two of coolies will be busy carrying out from the receiving store, and spreading not too thickly, but according to the weather, the parchment coffee for the day's drying on barbacues faced with bricks and tarred, having sufficient slope to run off rain water. In the evening of the second day it will be carried into another store near to the peeling-house, and next day spread out on a barbacue further up the yard, until by successive days' exposure it has become sufficiently dry and hard to be placed in the troughs of the peeling-mill and subjected to the rapid friction of the metal-faced wheels.

Thoroughly well dried parchment coffee is rapidly cleaned by being rubbed briskly between the hands, when the parchment falls into dust, and the beans are found ready for packing. The peeling-mill of the present day differs only from that of early times in being larger, better hung, more rapidly propelled, and of metal throughout with a corrugated face. The mechanical arrangements for removing the coffee and parchment dust, known as "chaff" from the mill, and separating them by means of fanners or winnowers, vary in different establishments, but in all the process is the same: so likewise we may say of the machinery for separating the beans of various sizes by means of sizers, and removing the pea-berry and broken beans, all of which are separately packed and marked: the means for effecting these objects are identically the same in all mills, but modified or combined with lifting apparatus, according to the requirements of each place.

In the early coffee days of Ceylon all that was done to the beans after being freed from the chaff was to pick out damaged or defective pieces: afterwards the pea-berries were removed by hand, and it was not until in more recent times that it was found worth while to size the coffee, an operation at first performed by hand, but eventually by sizers worked by steam power. The coffee curer has ascertained that the trifling additional cost of sizing is far more than compensated by the enhanced value of the coffee which is found to roast better when of even size. Greater care is also taken to remove from the sound portion of the sample every bean in the slightest degree injured, as it is found that the smallest cut from the pulper is apt to favor decay before reaching the home market, and seriously affect the flavor of the article.

The appliances for weighing and packing do not differ materially in any of the mills, nor does the preparation of the packages, in which great care is exercised, to the end that when turned out of the coolies' hands they may be not only sea-worthy, but coffee-worthy, in other words sound, strong, and sweet. A good charring in the inside of the cask will no doubt remove any slight resinous taint, but generally speaking, care is used to employ only good, sweet wood. How a sufficient supply is to be obtained ten years hence, at the present rate of consumption of eighty thousand casks a year, is one of those things no coffee curer can undertake to explain. Up to the year 1840 all coffee from Ceylon went home in bags; in that year a small experiment was made by shipping pea-berry in small boxes lined with paper: but this was a failure; the good woods were found too costly, and the cheap woods such as Hal and Dawata imparted an objectionable flavor to the contents. Ultimately kegs with the insides charred, were tried with success: then larger barrels, and eventually casks of six to nine hundredweights each.

Packed in casks of various sizes so as to secure better stowage, on ship-board, they are carefully marked with a view to placing the head-staves perpendicular when in the ship's hold, pressure above being found to damage the ends when this precaution is not taken. From the time the casks of coffee leave the mills, until they are on board ship, they do not part company with a stout tarpauline, so necessary is it that damp should not in any way penetrate the packages, and hence it is that, added to all the care that is given to our chief article of export within the mills, it is cared for up to its latest moments in Ceylon.

An account of our coffee mills would be manifestly imperfect without a slight sketch of the presiding genius, the store-keeper, who for many a year in olden days was master of the situation,

The original of the type I am about to describe, may be said to belong to a race nearly extinct in the present day: born of the necessities of their time, they have been gradually swept away by the necessities of a more advanced state of things, and are now only to be met with in the bye-ways of business, hanging on to the skirts of new comers unskilled in their filchings, and captivated by the low rate of salary with which they are content, as a cloak to daily and nightly swindles.

Your proper store-man is a Singhalese, but I could produce Malays fully as skilled in the craft of the professional store-keeper, as any "Tepanis" or "Juanis." In the early days of coffee in Ceylon, there were but few mills or stores that could afford the salary of a European manager, and it was moreover considered that on some such principle as that contained in the old saying of "set a thief to catch a thief," there was no person better able to work natives, than a native. This highly popular delusion obtained credence for a score of years, during which time the amount of fraud and peculation that was perpetrated through the Colombo coffee stores, was such as would have constitued a handsome fortune for most men, and actually did constitute a good many fortunes to the successful Tepanis's and Juanis's of the New Banffshire stores, and the United Channel Islanders' Mills of those ever to be lamented days, now all dead and gone. As the rings on the cocoanut tree indicate the age of the palm, so the jewellery and the general mounting of our model store-keeper, are pretty safe indications of his years in the profession. The first two years of his toils and depredation at the mills, are marked by pearl bnttons and tortoiseshell sleeve-links in his jacket and linen, a bullock hackery being his then ordinary mode of conveyance; the third and fourth years form the silver age of "Tepanis" when sleeve links and buttons of that metal supplant pearl, when the pony carriage replaces the hackery: gold buttons, a watch and chain, a horse and carriage, mark the last and crowning stage of the successful store-keeper, the horse being required not so much to convey him daily to and from the stores, as to carry him to the Cinnamon gardens, to superintend the building of the block of extensive dwelling-houses, which his "savings" have enabled him to erect at considerable outlay.

As with the growth and expansion of all other industries, there have been cycles and gradations in this branch of our local industries, fructifying to the especial advantage of Tepanis and his like. In the days of store-keepers' simplicity, when they served their employers, even as the house dog his master, they were content with the trifling fee in copper coin invariably extracted from the palms of Singhalese toilers, on each weekly pay-day, trifling in detail but important in the solid aggregate of accumulated pay-day fruits. There was not much to be said against this practice: at any rate though vicious in principle all contributed alike, and none would have performed a better day's work if freed from the small exactions. It formed a pretty addition to the humble salary of the store-keeper, so humble indeed that employers must have had strange ideas of the purchasing powers of thirty rix-dollars monthly, in the hands of their native subordinate, gaily decked as he was and gorgeously attired when on New Year's Day, he and all his belongings, paid their annual visit to the head of the farm as in duty bound, in all the glory of walking rainbows.

As years rolled on so passed away the simplicity of the primitive store-keepers, and their morality, ever elastic, underwent a change for the worse. The small copper coins were found two insignificant, for the enlarged ideas of Tepanis and his fellows. Silver was coveted, but silver could not be had from the weekly recipients of wages, and so the indigenous ingenuity of the race sought for it in another direction, where fine veins of the precious metal were quickly found, constituting an ever yielding el-dorado, veritable diggings of apparently prolific yield. This rich vein of metal was worked pretty much as follows:—cartmen and boatmen bringing coffee from the interior to the stores, were almost invariably short in their deliveries, sometimes very much so, occasionally only to a small extent; for this a deduction had to be made from their hire, and it was therefore, only a question of amount of the compromise to be arrived at between the measurer of coffee and the carriers, in order to arrange the little difference and secure for the latter a clean receipt and full balance of hire. Of course when coffee advanced in price, the inducement to sell the parchment on the way, was so much the greater, and in such cases the store-keeper was treated more liberally in the matter of fees. It may seem strange to some of our readers, that this system of bare-faced fraud has never been exposed, when it is known that the owners of stores, or their European office assistants, in their daily morning visits to the mills, failed to detect the cheat, as it was the custom to see any recently arrived lots of coffee measured in their presence, occasionally, by way of check as they supposed, but in vain: the measurement invariably turned out rather better than usual, and so all suspicion was lulled. We remember a case which occurred many years ago, in which a coffee curer having been assured by a discharged coolie, that tricks were played, managed to have two bags of estate coffee secretly removed from one of the carts conveying it to the store, by the coolie in question. In the morning the parcel of coffee was found to have been measured and turned out correct in the bushels, though two bags were stated to be short in the tally. On finding this the proprietor of the store ordered the parcel to be re-measured before him expecting to find the quantity short, but not so, the number of bushels was found to tally exactly with that entered in the receipt, and the coffee curer was non-plussed. The affair is managed in this way: in order to prevent the possibility of detection, by occasional checks in the measurement by one of the principals, sufficient parchment was invariably taken from another lot to make up the correct quantity, and thus detection became impossible. But it will be said what about the out-turn of the various lots? If a certain number of bushels of parchment were being constantly received short, there must have been an eventual deficiency in the quantity of clean coffee shipped: this was what happened, and this fact fully explains the very irregular out-turn of estate coffee in those days, which was known to range between 4: 60 and 5: 50 bushels to the hundred weight. After a time these irregular results led to searching enquiries and unpleasant questioning, and so the wily store-keepers resorted to another dodge, in order to conceal the short receipts of parchment in their stores: they professed to ship more coffee than actually left their mills, by marking the casks in excess of their actual contents: some pounds on each cask, did not create suspicion, and on arrival in London the difference was supposed to have arisen from driage on the voyage home.

The trick of false marking has been known to have extended to the tare of the cask, which being marked on the packages less than it was, necessarily made it appear that there was more coffee in it than was actually the case, and this has been known to have been resorted to, in order to cover the weight of a quantity of good clean estate coffee removed from the mills during the day-time, under the pretence of it being black and having been sold to a confederate outside at a nominal figure, a little black coffee being placed on the top of each bag of the good. To what extent this latter system of robbery was carried on, it would be impossible to form any opinion, but there is no doubt that the total of the fraudulent gains of native store-keepers, and of some few not natives by birth, but by proclivities, has been very large indeed. We have been assured that frauds have been perpetrated in the measurement of coffee even when most rigorously watched by a European store-keeper of undoubted integrity: it has been managed by a confederate secreting himself behind a heap of bags of coffee in the evening, and being locked in all night, employing the short space of the early dawn in making up the deficiency in his lot, by abstraction from another parcel near at hand.

But there are sources of gain for the model store-keepers, other than in the bean itself. The stores have to be enlarged by the addition of another extensive wing, a new picking house, and a new upper-story, all of which involve a good deal of consultation between Maricar, the contractor, and Tepanis the store-keeper, generally on Sunday at the villa residence of the latter. The result of these diplomatic conference is, that Maricar obtains the contract after deducting a certain amount which had been added for the express purpose of being reduced by the zealous and faithful Tepanis in the interests of his respected employer. About the same period a new house is commenced in the Cotta road on a nice plot of ground acquired by the honest industry of Tepanis, the masonry work is done by Maricar's men, the bricks come from the same kiln as furnish the materials for the new store building, likewise the carpenter's work, and a year afterwards Tepanis astonishes his numerous circle of friends, by informing them what a ridiculously small sum that house cost him : they cannot imagine how it was done for the money, all except his younger brother, who puts his tongue in his cheek, and winks quietly at Tepanis as he drinks off another glass of that fine, nutty, after-dinner sherry of 1833, advertised at 22*s.* 6*d.* the dozen.

A NEW YEAR'S DAY.

THERE are some of our fellow-subjects in the East, who appear to have been rather unfairly dealt with by writers of Indian books, and colonial histories, inasmuch as no notice has been taken of them, save in the official census, in which, by the way, they figure rather prominently as regards number. I allude to the Burgher inhabitants of our large colonial towns within the tropics.

In Europe the term "Burgher" was applied, in olden days, to all citizens or dwellers in principal towns, carrying on trades or professions therein. In the East, or rather within the tropics, it is used to designate the decendants of the old Portuguese and Dutch colonists, a class at once numerous and respectable. At the Cape Colony they form the majority of settlers; but in the tropical settlements of Ceylon, Singapore, etc., they are outnumbered by other races. When the former island was taken possession of by the British forces, many of the Dutch civil servants returned to Holland or migrated to Java; but very many lacked the means to travel, or preferred remaining where they had been born. Their descendants have continued to fill many leading posts in the colonial establishments, and nearly all the minor appointments in the judicial and revenue departments are bestowed upon these and the Portuguese Burghers. The Dutch have been, and are to this day very careful not to intermarry with any Singhalese; thus their habits and their characters have undergone but little change. The Portuguese, on the other hand, have been far less scrupulous on this point; and their descendants of the present day are to be seen of every shade and grade, from the well-clad medical student, to the half starved, ill-clad mechanic or the indolent bazaar-keeper.

If the English colonists contrive to monopolize the best berths in the service, the Burghers have managed to secure to themselves the most comfortable dwellings, with the best gardens. The same jealous exclusiveness which has so completely separated these two classes, impels the European to take up his residence in a quarter as far removed as possible from the suburbs usually occupied by the Burghers. The English merchants and civil servants will be found located along the edge of some high road, within a very small patch of burnt-up paddock. Their tenements are of no particular order, being mostly long rambling whitewashed places. A few palms make an attempt at shading the hot verandah in front: while the small tufts of cinnamon bushes are to be seen struggling for life in parched sand, evidently disgusted with their circumstances. How different the dwellings of the Burghers! Some of these, it is true, are in the midst of the Pettah or native town, but most of them will be found scattered about in quiet, shady lanes. Many are quite hidden from the passer-by, amidst dense little clusters of fruit-trees, rose bushes, and evergreens—concealed amidst leaves and flowers as snugly as though they were so many huge, red-bricked, bird's nests.

It is seldom, indeed that anything occurs to break the dull monotony of life in the East. With few public amusements, no promenades, colonists seldom meet each other save in their churches. There are however, a few days in the year when a little change in this clock-work existence takes place amongst the Burgher population; when hard visaged Dutchmen relax the stern rigidity of their bronzed features, and put on some gay suit of many colors. When portly dames rouse up for the emergency, startle the quiet family halls with their busy tongues, and scare the old house-dog with the vivid brilliancy of bright ribands and new lace.

One of these very few and much prized occasions is New Year's Day.

In the afternoon of the first day in January, 1850, I strolled out from the old sturdy fort of Colombo, over a lumbering wooden drawbridge, through some of the broad, prim-looking streets of the native town. The bland sea-breeze played coyly with the feathery foliage of the tall palms and arekas, and waved against the azure sky many a tope of broad-leaved, bright-green bananas. Away upon the breezy ocean far out from land, a little fleet of fishing canoes were

discernable making their swift way to shore with welcome loads, the toilers of the deep eager to be with their friends and join in the glad rejoicings of that welcome New Year's Day. The native bazaar, at the corner of the town, with one end jutting out upon the sea, was for once clean and gay. The dealers in fish, fruit, and curry-stuffs appeared to have put on new clothes with the New Year. The huge white turbans, and gilt-edged muslin scarfs, glistened in the noon-day sun; and gorgeous, many coloured vests and wrappers vied, in the brilliancy of their tints with the piles of many-hued fruits and balmy flowers. The very fish and vegetables appeared cleaner than usual; while spices, condiments and sweetmeats looked down from many a loaded shelf upon the passer-by.

Leaving this motley scene, I passed on to the heart of the dwelling-place of the middle-class of Burghers. Before every house was an ample verandah partly veiled by an open bamboo-curtain. In these lofty, cool retreats were seated the many families of the place, receiving or giving the good wishes of the season. Once upon a time the streets were graced by rows, on either side of shady spreading sooriya-trees bending over the footways, and peeping in at the verandahs, to see how the inmates were getting on; winking the large eyes of their yellow tulip flowers at the daughters, and enticing pretty birds to come and sing amongst the leafy branches. But this was in the good old days of sleepy Holland. Now all are gone—green boughs, winking flowers, and singing-birds: more's the pity!

As I passed along I met many groups of old, young and middle-aged, evidently families, in full native holiday costume. They were in each case followed by two or more turbaned, fierce-looking domestics, bearing enormous trays piled up with something hidden from vulgar gaze by flowing veils of muslin. I could not help calling to mind the processions of slaves in the Arabian Nights, which we are informed followed the steps of caliphs and sorcerers, bearing with them huge presents of precious things from subterranean worlds. I watched some of these domestic embassies and perceived that they entered the houses of some of the neighbours; there was a great fluster and bustle, and no end to talking and laughing in the long verandahs. I entered the dwelling of Dutchman to whom I was known, and found one of these family groups within. A rare merry scene it was: the deputation had just arrived; friends were shaking hands; the great black slave of the Arabian Nights uncovered the hidden treasures on the tray, and, lo! there were discovered —not piles of glittering sequins, and emeralds, and rubies, as I had expected, but a few bunches of yellow plantains, some green oranges, a handful of limes, half-a-dozen pine-apples, and a homely-looking cake frosted with sugar. These were the universal New Year offerings amongst that simple community, given as tokens of good-fellowship and neighbourly feelings; and as such, welcomed and cheerfully responded to. Little corpulent glasses of cordials, or schiedam, were handed round amongst all arrivals, rich or poor; good wishes were exchanged; a few stale jokes were cracked; inquiries were made for the grandmother who was too infirm to join the party; and away went the neighbours with another slave and another heap of hidden gifts, to the next acquaintance. These presents are not confined to mere equals; the most humble menial scrapes a few challies together for the occasion and lays at his master's feet an oblation of fruits and flowers.

The very grass-cutter, the miserable hanger-on of stables, contrives somehow to get a few pines and plantains on a blue-and-white dish; and poverty-stricken though she be, pours out her simple gifts before her master, with gentle dignity.

Group after group went through the town. Gay parties continued to amuse themselves in many a dusty verandah. Scores of meerschaums sent forth circling clouds of fragrant white smoke; while many a dreamy Dutchman nodded in his high-backed, richly-carved chair of ebony. The hour of vespers approached. There were heard dozens of tinkling little bells; and forth came scores of damsels clad in pure white. Again the dusty streets were busy and alive, and many of the good Catholic verandahs lost their chief charmers.

Straying onward from this bustling neighbourhood, I reached the outskirts of the town, where are to be seen some of the prettiest and most retired of the Burghers' dwellings. These are mostly fine old mansions of red brick, with solid, grim-looking gable-ends frowning down upon the old rusty gates, and the great round wall by the forest of plantain-trees. I found myself standing before one of these, in a sweet green lane lined with lofty palms, spreading gorekas, and huge india-rubber trees. The heavy wall in front hid the sturdy mansion from my view; but the gates being open, I obtained a peep of the oriental paradise within. Rare old fruit-trees on the grass-plot were well laden with clustering, many-coloured fruit! They must have been in bearing when the old gentleman in the easy chair, and the pink cotton trousers, and black skull-cap, was a mere child. How cool the place looked amidst all that dense green foliage! One might almost have caught a cold in the head by merely looking in at the gate: the sun evidently never troubled the little children playing on the grass under the thick cluster of mangoes, sour-sops, and plantains except, perhaps, for a few minutes at noon. What a jolly old house it was, to be sure, with verandahs as large as the Burlington Arcade in London; and such windows! They looked like so many roofs of hot-houses let sideways into the walls; and as for the doors, one might have fancied, from their size, that the family were in the habit of keeping their carriage in the back parlour, or setting out the dinner-table in the doorway: there would have been abundance of room in either case, and a little to spare too!

There were nice beds of flowers on each side of the large grass-plot, and orange trees; and the passer-by peeping in far enough, as I did, might have caught a glimpse of one or two pairs of small pretty feet, and faces to match, hidden away cosily among the roses and oleanders. Well, these are nice, quiet, enjoyable places, and much better than the hot, dusty, dignified rabbit-hutches of the English on the other side of the fort!

I passed on as my fancy led me, until I came to another stout Dutch residence, which pleased me though not so much as the other had done. It was altogether another description of house, though doubtless pleasant enough in its way. It stood close upon the road with all the garden behind it, so that one saw nothing but red bricks and little Dutch tiles.

There was no peeping in there, through any open gates; no catching the daughters quietly among the flowers.

The owner of the house chanced to be enjoying his pipe in the capacious doorway; and seeing me surveying the premises, he at once rose from his quiet seat and bade me welcome. When he learnt my desire to examine his mansion, he gladly conducted me through the building to the garden. The principal room or hall was of great size. I believe you might have driven a stage-coach, with very frisky leaders, round the dinner-table, without fear of touching the army of chairs ranged along the walls. I could almost fancy the builder had made a mistake, and roofed in a good part of the road. I looked up, and when at length I discovered the roof, I wondered whether the sparrows building their nests so high there, ever felt giddy and fell down and killed themselves upon the tiled floor. The other rooms were less ample, but all spacious enough, and well filled with ebony and calamander furniture. There was a degree of polish about the windows, and a sort of rakishness in the couch-covers and ottoman drapery, which filled me with admiration; while the very screen in the doorway had a jaunty air about it which there was no resisting.

Right and left from the large house, extended backward two ranges of sleeping apartments and stores, with long stone terraces, filled with flowering shrubs in gigantic pots. At the farther end were rows of huge, suspiciously-shaped jars, looking as though they belonged to Ali Baba and the Forty Thieves. At the termination of this pottery were wide flights of steps leading to a neatly laid-out garden, full of the richest flowers, and greenest shrubs, and most tempting fruit trees the eye ever saw, or fancy pictured. There was a small fountain in the midst, with a seat by the side, and round it lay scattered children's toys. On the whole, this was a pretty place, but not so natural and home-like as the other; besides, the stiff terrace and the jars of the Forty Thieves rather marred its natural beauty, whilst adding to its air of romance.

The evening was magnificent. A young and lovely moon flung many a pale ray of light among the gorgeous foliage that danced in the cool sea-breeze. The vast Indian Ocean broke peacefully in phosphorescent waves curling upon a pebbly shore. The air was soft and still, broken only by fitful echoes from some merry-making party in the distance.

My drive home led me by the sea-shore, and, as I gazed out upon the far ocean, I noticed a little black shadow on the horizon, like a ship, or as the shadow of some monstrous winged thing. Tired of watching, I lay back and dozed. I looked out again, and started to find how dark it had become. The horse-keeper, too, was urging the animal to its utmost speed. The little black speck on the horizon had swollen to a mighty, hideous mass of thunder-cloud. Already half the heavens were shrouded in pitchy darkness. I opened my carriage window and looked out. The storm was coming up with giant strides; some distance out at sea, a wall of smoking, hissing, bubbling rain joined the clouds and ocean, and shut out all beyond. I could hear that mighty cataract of tempest fall with a roaring sound, nearer and nearer. Before me, all was dark and stormy: behind, the many groves of waving palms still slept in early moon-light beauty. The distant hills were clear and bold, and seemed so near, as though my voice could reach them.

It was in vain my horse was urged onward: the storm was swifter than any living thing. The great black smoking wall came hissing on; and from its darkened crest, loud peals of thunder burst. I have been in many a storm in my day, but this was the most magnificent I ever beheld. To go onward became absolutely impossible; so fierce was the tempest. The driver therefore turned the horse's head away from the sea, and patiently sat it out. Peal after peal of thunder rent the air. It seemed as though all the powder-magazines in the world were being blown up. First there was a cracking and splitting, as of gigantic sheets of metal torn asunder ; then a heavy tumbling like ten thousand loaded waggons being galloped across an iron bridge. The air was no longer darkened; every foot of atmosphere seemed alive with lightning-life. By the glare, I could see some of the noble palms —at least seventy feet high—bending to the gale like willow wands, and literally sweeping the ground with their feathery leaves. More than one, upon that terrible night, was shivered into splinters by the lightning; and many a stubborn one that would not bend, lay crushed and helpless on its sandy grave.

The howling of the wind, the thunder-peals, the heavy pattering of the huge rain-drops, had well-nigh stunned me. In nature, however, as with man, the fiercest outbreaks are the soonest quelled. In half an hour the moon shone out again in undimmed beauty. The air was calm and hushed; and the parched earth and herbs, grateful for such a copious draught, sent many a fragrant blessing on the breeze, to tell their thanks.

OUR NATIONAL TREE.

TO dwellers in Ceylon, the cocoanut palm calls up a wide range of ideas; it associates itself with nearly every want, and convenience of native life. It might tempt a Singhalese villager to assert that if he were placed upon the earth with nothing else whatever to minister to his necessities than the cocoanut tree, he could pass his existence in happiness and contentment.

When he has felled one of these trees after it has ceased bearing (say in its seventieth year), with its trunk he builds his hut and his bullock-stall, which he thatches with its leaves. His bolts and bars are slips of the bark; by which he also suspends the small shelf which holds his stock of home-made utensils and vessels. He fences his little plot of chillies, tobacco, and fine grain, with the leaf-stalks. The infant is swung to sleep in a rude net of coir-string made from the husk of the fruit; its meal of rice and scraped cocoanut is boiled over a fire of cocoanut shells and husks, and is eaten off a dish formed of the plaited green leaves of the tree, with a spoon cut out of the nut-shell. When he goes a-fishing by torch-light his net is of cocoanut fibre, the torch, or chule is a bundle of dried cocoanut leaves and flower-stalks: the little canoe is the trunk of the cocoa-palm tree, hollowed by his own hands. He carries home his net and string of fish on a yoke, or pingo, formed of a cocoanut stalk. When he is thirsty, he drinks of the fresh juice of the young nut; when he is hungry, he eats its soft kernel. If he have a mind to be merry, he sips a glass of arrack, distilled from the fermented juice, and he flavours his curry with vinegar made from this toddy. Should he be sick, his body will be rubbed with cocoanut oil; he sweetens his coffee with jaggery, or cocoanut sugar, and softens it with cocoanut milk; it is sipped by the light of a lamp, constructed from a cocoanut shell, and fed by cocoanut oil. His doors, his windows, his shelves, his chairs, the water-gutter under the eaves, all are made from the wood of the tree. His spoons, his forks, his basins, his mugs, his salt-cellars, his jars, his child's money-box, are all constructed from the shell of the nut. Over his couch when first born, and over his grave when buried, a bunch of cocoanut blossoms is hung, to charm away evil spirits.

This palm is assiduously cultivated in Ceylon, in topes, or plantations; and it was long believed that the rude native system of culture was the best: but experience has shown the fallacy of this opinion. Hence, the Singhalese continue to find the manual labor, but the Englishman provides skill and implements.

There is a good road to within a couple of miles of the plantation I am about to describe; so that the visitor has little difficulty in performing this much of the journey. The remaining two miles lie through a sandy track of very flat and rather uninteresting country. Here and there, amidst a maze of paddy fields, arecanut topes, and patches of low thorny jungle, are dotted little white-walled huts. They are much cleaner than any such near the towns of Ceylon; attached to each is a small slip of ground, rudely fenced, and half cultivated, with a few sweet potatoes, some chillies, and a little tobacco and fine grain. It was midday when I started, on foot, to this estate. The sun was blazing above in unclouded glory. Under the shade of a breadfruit tree, the owner of the first hut I got to was dozing and chewing betel-nut, evidently tasting, in anticipation, the bliss of Buddha's paradise. The wife was pounding up something for curry; the children were by her side—the boys smoking tiny cheroots, the girls twisting mats. It was fortunate for me that the sandy path was over-shadowed by jungle trees, or my progress would have been impossible. Not a breath of air was stirring amidst that dense mass of vegetation; not a twig or a leaf could be persuaded to move; the long and graceful paddy stalks glittered and sparkled in their watery resting places, as though they were made of the purest burnished silver. The buffaloes had taken to their noon-day watering places. The birds were evidently done up, and were nowhere to be seen; the beetles crawled feebly over the cooler shrubs, but they could not get up a single hum or a buzz amongst them all; even the busy little ants perspired, and dropped their lilliputian loads. Well, the dry ditch and thorny fence that form the boundary and protection of the estate were at least reached, and the little gate and watch-hut were passed. The watcher, or lascoryn, was a Malay, moustachioed and fierce; for the natives of the country can rarely be depended on as protectors of property against their fellow-villagers. A narrow belt of jungle trees and shrubs had been left quite round the plantation, to assist in keeping out cattle and wild animals, which are frequently very destructive to a young cocoanut estate, in spite of armed watchers, ditches, and fences. Passing through this little belt, I found, on entering, an entirely new scene: before and around me waved gracefully the long shining leaves of three hundred acres of cocoanut palms, each acre containing, on an average, eighty trees. It was indeed a beautiful and interesting sight. Two-thirds of these trees were yielding ample crops, though only in their tenth year; in two years more they will, generally, be in full bearing. Unlike the rudely planted native garden, this estate had been most carefully laid down; the young plants had all been placed out at regular intervals and in perfectly straight lines, so that, looking over the estate in either direction, the long avenues presented one unbroken figure, at once pleasing to the eye and easy of access. But if these interminable masses of palms appeared a lovely picture, when regarded at some little distance, how much was their beauty heightened on a nearer inspection! Walking close under the shadow of their long and ribbon-like leaves, I could see how thickly they were studded with golden-green fruit, in every stage of growth. The sight was absolutely marvellous: were such trees, so laden, painted by an artist, his production would, in all probability, be pronounced unnatural. They appeared more like some fairy creations, got up for my special amusement, resembling nearly those gorgeous trees which, in my youth, I delighted to read about in the Arabian Nights, growing in subterranean gardens, and yielding precious stones. They hung in grape-like clusters around the crest of the tree; the large golden ripe nuts below, smaller and greener fruit just above them, followed by scores of others in all stages, from the blossom-seed to the half-grown; it was impossible to catch a glimpse of the stem, so thickly did the fruit hang on all sides. I made an attempt to count them:—"thirty—fifty—eighty—one hundred"—I could go no further; those little fellows near the top, peeping up like so many tiny dolls' heads, defied my most careful numeration; but I feel confident there must have been quite two hundred nuts on that one palm. Above the clusters of rich fruit were two feather-like flowers, white as snow, and smooth and glossy as polished ivory; they had just burst from their sheaths; and a more delicate, lovely picture could scarcely be imagined.

A cocoanut tree in a native Singhalese tope, will sometimes yield fifty nuts in twelve months; but the average of them seldom give more than twenty-five in the year. It is therefore very evident that European skill may be employed beneficially on this cultivation, as well as on any other.

I was at first rather startled at perceiving a tall, half-naked Singhalese away in the distance, with a gun at least half as long again as himself, long black hair over his shoulders, and bunches of something hanging at his girdle. He was watching some game amongst the trees; at last he fired, ran, picked up something, and stuck it in his girdle. What could it be?

Parrot, pigeon, or jungle-fowl? It was only a poor little squirrel; and there were at least two scores of these pretty creatures hanging at the waist of the mighty hunter! Fortunately, I could speak the native language, and was not long in learning the cause of this slaughter. It appeared that in addition to their pretty bushy tails, glossy coats, and playful gambols, the squirrels have very sharp and active teeth, and an uncommon relish for the sweet tender buds of the cocoanut flower, which they nip off and destroy by scores, and of course lessen by so much, the future crop of fruit. Handsfull of the buds lay half-eaten around each tree, and I no longer felt astonished at this species of sporting.

The ground had evidently been well cleared from jungle plants, not one of which was to be seen in all this track: a stout and healthy-looking grass was springing up along the avenues; whilst at intervals, patches of Indian corn, sweet potatoes, guinea-grass, and other products—intended for cattle-fodder during dry weather when the wild grasses fail—gave tints of varied luxuriance to the scene.

The ground at this part of the estate sloped a little, and I came to an open space, somewhat marshly in appearance. A number of cattle, young and old, were browsing about on the long grass, or sipping a draught from the clear stream which ran through the low ground. They were confined within a rude but stout fence, and on one side was a range of low sheds for their shelter. The cattle appeared in good condition; they were purchased, when very young, from the drovers who bring them in hundreds from the Malabar coast; and many were then fit for the cart, the carriage, or the knife. At the end was a manure shed, and outside stood a keeper's hut, with a store attached, in which were piled up dried guinea-grass, maize, etc.

The manure-pit was deep and large, and in it lay the true secret of the magical productiveness of the trees I had just seen. Good seed planted in light free soil, well cleared and

and drained, will produce a fine healthy tree in a few years; and if to this be added occasional supplies of manure and a few waterings during the dry season, an abundant yield of fruit will most assuredly reward the toil and outlay of the cocoa-nut cultivator.

Leaving this spot, I strolled through the next field, to see what a number of little boys were so busy about. There were a dozen dark urchins, running about from tree to tree; sometimes they stopped, clambered up, and appeared to have very particular business to transact at the stems of the leaves; but oftener they passed contented with a mere glance upwards at the fruit. They had a sharp-pointed instrument in the hand: whilst at the wrist of each was hung a cocoanut shell. I paused to see what one of these children was searching for half hid as the little fellow was amongst the gigantic leaves. Intently scrutinizing his motions, I observed that he forced the little sharp instrument into the very body of the tree: down it went to the inmost core of the giant stem: all his strength was employed; he strained and struggled amongst the huge leaves as though he were engaged in deadly strife with some terrible boa or cheetah. At last he secured his antagonist, and descended with something alive, small and black, and impaled on the barbed point of the little weapon: a few questions elicited the whole secret. The cocoanut tree, it seems, has many enemies besides squirrels: the elephant, the wild hog, the rat, the white ant, the porcupine, the monkey, and a large white worm, either attack it when young, or rob it of its fruit when mature. But the most numerous and persevering enemy which it has to encounter from the age of three years until long after it produces fruit, is *cooroominiya*, or cocoanut beetle; a black, hard-coated creature, with beautiful wings, and a most powerful little tusk, which it employs with fatal activity to open a way into the stems of the palms. Its labours commence in the evening, and by early morning it will be buried half-a-dozen inches deep in the very centre of the tree, where, if not detected and removed, it feeds on the soft pithy fibres, deposits its eggs, and does not depart in less than two or three days. These holes are always made in the softest and sweetest part of the tree, near the crown; and in young plants they prove seriously hurtful; checking the growth, and impairing the health of the future tree. In a morning's walk an active lad will frequently secure as many as a score of these *cooroominiyas*, which, after being killed, are strung upon lilliputian gibbets about the estate, as a warning to their live friends.

Farther on I perceived, gathered in anxious consultation, three of the lads around a tree that was loaded with fruit; they looked up at the leaves, then at the root, then at the trunk. At last one little fellow started off, swift-footed as a hare, and was soon out of sight. The others began scraping the earth from the root as fast as possible; and all the information they would impart was "*ledde gaha*," or sick tree; so that there was nothing for it but to imagine that the little messenger had been despatched for the doctor. He soon came back, not with the medicine-man, but a *mamootie*, or Dutch hoe, and a *cattie*, or sharp bill-hook. And then the busy work went on again. In little more time than I take to tell the story, the soil was removed from about the root, a hole was discovered in the trunk, and its course upwards ascertained by means of a cane probe. With the *cattie*, one of the boys commenced cutting and opening midway in the trunk of the tree. On looking up, I perceived that the patient gave unmistakeable symptoms of ill-health. The long leaves were drooping at the end, and tinged with a sickly yellow; many of the nuts had fallen off, and others had evidently half a mind to follow the example. The flower, which had just burst above, hung down its sickly head, weeping away the germs of what had else been fruit. The hole was now complete; it was large enough for the smallest boy to force his hand in; and it soon brought away a basket-full of pith and powdered wood from the body of the tree. There, amidst the ruin, was the enemy that has caused so much mischief and labour. It was an unsightly worm, about four inches in length, and as thick as one's small finger, having a dull white body and black head. I then began to wonder what had next to be done, whether the tree would die after all this hacking and maiming. Would the medicine-man now be sent for? No. The interior of the wounded tree, as well as the aperture, was thoroughly freed from dirt and decomposed fibre—which might have aided in hatching any eggs left by the worm—and finally the root was covered up, and the opening and inside of the palm tightly filled with clay. I was assured that not more than one of ten trees, thus treated, ever fails to recover its health.

The nocturnal attacks of elephants are checked by means of lighted fires, and an occasional shot or two during the night. Wild hogs and porcupines are caught in traps, and hunted by dogs. The monkeys are shot down like the squirrels, and the white ants are poisoned. In spite of all these measures, however, an estate often suffers very severely, and its productiveness is much interfered with by these depredators.

The soil over which I had as yet passed had been of one uniform description—a light sandy earth, containing a little vegetable matter, and but a little. Afterwards I arrived at a tract of planted land, quite different in its nature and mode of cultivation. It was of a far stiffer character, deeper in colour, and more weedy. This portion of the estate was in former days a swamp, in which the porcupine, the wild hog, and the jackal, delighted to dwell, sheltered from the encroachment of man by a dense mass of low jungle, thorns, and reeds. To drive away these destructive creatures from the vicinity of the young palms, the jungle was fired, during dry weather. It was then perceived that the soil of this morass, although wet and rank from its position, was of a most luxuriant character; a few deep drains were opened through the centre, cross drains were cut, and after one season's exposure to the purifying action of the atmosphere and rain, the whole of it was planted, and it now gives fair promise of being one day the finest field in the plantation.

From this low ground I strolled through some long avenues of trees on the right; their long leaves protected me from the heat of the afternoon sun, which was still considerable. The trees on this side were evidently older: they had a greater number of ripe fruit; and further away in the distance might be seen a multitude of men and boys busily engaged in bearing away the huge nuts in pairs, to a path or rude cart track, where a *cangany*, or native overseer, was occupied in counting them as they were tossed into the bullock cart. The expertness of the boys in climbing these smooth, lofty and branchless trees, by the aid of a small band formed by twisting a portion of a cocoanut leaf, was truly astonishing. In a moment their small feet grasped the trunk, aided by the twisted leaf, whilst their hands were employed above; they glided upwards, and with a quick eye detected the riper fruit, which, rapidly twisted from their stalks, were flung to the ground. Their companions below were busy in removing the nuts, which for young children is no easy task; the nuts frequently weighing fifteen or twenty pounds each, with the husk or outer skins on them. The natives have a simple but ingenious method of tying them together in pairs, by which means the boys can carry two of them with ease, when otherwise one would be a task of difficulty. The nuts have little, if any, stalk: the practice therefore is to slit up a portion of the husk (which is the coir fibre in its natural state), pull out a sufficient length without breaking it, and thus tie two together; in this way the little urchins scamper along with the nuts slung across their shoulders, scarcely feeling the weight.

I followed the loaded carts. They were halted at a large enclosure, inside of which were huge pens formed of jungle sticks, about ten feet in height; into these the nuts were stored and recounted; a certain number only being kept in each, as the pens are all of the same dimensions. Adjoining, was another and still larger space, lying lower, with some deep ditches and pits in the midst. Here the outer husk is stripped off, preparatory to breaking the nut itself in order to obtain the kernel, which has to be dried before the oil can be expressed. Into the pits or ditches the husk is flung, and left in water ten or fourteen days, when it is removed and beaten out on stones, to free the elastic fibre from dirt and useless vegetable matter. This is a most disagreeable operation, for the stench from the half-putrid husks is very strong. The fibre, after being well dried on the sandy ground, undergoes a rude assortment into three qualities, in reference chiefly to colour, and is then delivered over to the rope maker, who works it up into yarn, rope, or junk, as required. Freed from their outer covering, the nuts, are either sold for making curries, in which they form a prominent feature, or they are kept for drying ready for the oil-mill.

Having learned this much, I strolled through the small green field and along a patch of guinea-grass, to see what was going on in that direction. The neat-looking building adjoining was the superintendent's bungalow, and the long sheds and open spaces in their front and rear were for drying the nuts into what is termed *copperah*, in which state they are ground up for pressure. It was a busy scene indeed, and the operations require constant vigilance on the part of the manager; yet all the work is carried on in the rudest way, and with the most simple implements. Half-a-dozen stout lads were seated cross-legged on the ground, each with a heap of nuts by his side. The rapidity with which they seized these, and, with one sharp blow of a heavy knife, split them precisely in half, and flung them away into other heaps, was remarkable. It seemed to be done with scarcely an effort: yet on handling the broken nut, one could not help being struck with its thickness and strength. Smaller boys were busily employed in removing these heaps of split fruit to the large open spaces, where others, assisted by a few women, were occupied in placing them in rows close together, with the open part upwards, so that the kernels may be fully exposed to the direct rays of the sun. In this way they remain for two day, when the fruit partly dried, shrinks from the shell, and is removed. Two more days' exposure to the sun in fine weather, will generally complete the drying process. The kernels are then called *copperah*, and are brittle and unctuous in the hand.

To convert this material into oil, the natives employ a very primitive mill, worked by bullocks, and called a *checkoo*; this process is very slow, and the oil never clean. Europeans have however obviated these objections, and manufacture the cocoanut oil by means of granite crushers and hydraulic presses worked by steam power. This is chiefly done in Colombo, to which place of course the *copperah* has to be conveyed. The refuse of the oil-presses, the dry cake or *poonac*, is very useful as food for cattle or poultry, and not less so as a manure for the palm-trees, when moistened, and applied in a partially decomposed state.

Not a particle of this valuable tree is lost. The fresh juice of the blossom, which is broken off to allow it to flow freely, is termed, as we have said, toddy, and is drunk, when quite new, as a cool and pleasantly refreshing beverage; when fermented, it is distilled, and yields the less harmless liquor known as arrack.

All these operations are not carried on with ease and regularity. The Singhalese are an idle race; like many better men, their chief pleasure is to perform as little work as possible. This necessitates a never-ending round of inspection by the European manager, who, mounted on a small pony, paper umbrella in hand, visits every corner of the property at least once in a day, often twice. Neither is it unusual for him to make "a round" during the night. On the whole therefore, he enjoys no sinecure.

THE KANDYANS' CAPTIVE.

NEVER had sun shone brighter, or sky looked more serenely blue and heaven-like, or early morning-breeze breathed softer, or palm trees waived more gracefully, or flowers looked more sweetly, than sun, and sky, and breeze, and palms and flowers on morning of the Christmas day of which I write, in the ninth year from the opening of this century, when Kandy looked from where our captive saw it, with palace at his feet and town stretched far away, like a tiled citadel amidst a fort of straw.*

Above the town of Kandy on a grassy knoll, just in the rear of the present pavilion grounds, not far above where stands the Judges' bungalow, was at the time I write, a small building placed amidst a tope of trees as a bird would hide its nest. The hut, for it was little else, was looped around with creeping, flowering plants, and on the little grassy knoll before it were groups of roses, jasmin and other tropical flowers, giving evidence of more than native care and taste. Beneath a spreading tamarind tree, the captive of the Kandyan monarch sat, a pale and thoughtful man, gazing out on the hills that faced him on the west, thinking of Christmas in Old England, of Christmas where the yule-log blazed, and where those whom he never more should see, his children, played, laughed, and wondered why he did not come.

The captive was not alone. At his feet just as a petted spaniel, sat a young girl with folded hands and thoughtful face, knowing well his wandering thoughts and knowing how

---

* Under native rule none but the royal buildings and Temples were allowed to be constructed of stone, brick and tiles: all others were of mud thatched with straw.

vain for him though not for her, content to let him think and gaze in silence. The little house was decorated with ferns and roses and many flowers taken prisoners from the woods by Lenna's hand in honour of the day, the Christians' greatest festival.

Six years had passed since the fearful tragedy which placed the captive in the Kandyan's hand: those years had told heavily upon him. Horror, remorse, grief, terror, had at length given place to resignation. He had brought himself to feel that in his lonely prison-life, he had to expiate the one sad error, costing how many lives. Five years of the six had been past in still drearier solitude, in one of the royal prisons near Badulla.* His confinement at first close though not rigorous, had been gradually relaxed until he was left unguarded. By degrees he had acquired the native tongue from that most teachable of all agencies, female lips. The young daughter of the chief to whose care he was confided, took womanly pity on his loneliness, and did much to lighten the sadness of his captivity. From her he had learnt the first words of native language, and in turn instructed her in English.

The girl was quicker than the man, and long before he could make himself clearly understood in the vernacular, she could talk to him in Oriental Saxon. The key to language once found the rest soon came: *the book* which had never left his hands, which was his daily study, that book was an object of her curiosity. By slow degrees, almost word by word, he told her the good tidings in that volume. He related the wonderous history that it chronicled. He taught her from the precepts of its pages, until they thought as one and read together.

---

* In the days of the Kandyan Sovereigns there were three places to which the prisoners were transported, one near Badulla, for light offenders of rank; one in the Seven Korales, for criminals of a deeper dye; and a third, in the Bintenna district immediately below Lagalla. Transportation to this locality was equivalent to death, as it was then so pestilential, that none who went there were known to return.

During his banishment to Badulla repeated messages had reached him from the king, inquiring of his health, wants and wishes, sometimes making tempting offers if he would forswear allegiance to his sovereign. At length the order had gone forth to remove him to the capital. It was a long and weary journey in those days from Badulla to Kandy: a chair on poles conveyed him to the royal city. Lenna would not remain behind, and so the litter was given up to her when the road lay through rugged or steep places, and when they came to pleasant smooth sward, she walked by his side, and thus they came to Kandy where the king received his captive graciously. Five years of peace had soothed the tyrant, and he bade his nobles lodge their prisoner where he pleased, and so he chose the hill-side knoll whence he could look towards the west. Twelve months in Kandy had reconciled him somewhat to his captive life, and in frequent interviews with the royal despot he found more disposition to shew kindness so that sometimes he began to hope. His Majesty had learnt the season of the Christian's Festival had arrived, and it was his gracious pleasure that the day should be a holiday, and that he would in proper state give audience to the English officer in the great "Hall of Seals."* The audience hall on ordinary occasions was the building now used as the District Court, immediately facing the Kutcherry which was then a portion of the royal palace. On special occasions, such as the present, the reception was in the Hall of Seals, a lofty open building on the ground where now stands the Kandy Girls' School, adjoining the Dewale, and facing the esplanade on which there was ample room for the royal troops to be paraded. The house now occupied by the Government Agent was used as a Hall of Spectacle † from the windows of which the Queen and

---

* So called from its being the place in which all presents from vassals or foreign rulers were deposited, and where their seals were broken.

† Davy mentions this building (Chap. X. p. 321) as the Queen's palace: but this according to my informant, was incorrect.

ladies of the household could witness all public festivities, or as the case might be, public executions, which in those days were scenes of protracted barbarity. The royal executioner, the king's elephant, was kept close by, ready to do his horrid bidding at a word or sign.

It was in the morning of this day, the captive and his companion were gazing from beneath their favorite tamarind tree: he looked towards the west, and then gazed down upon the busy scene below, upon the gay streamers and many-colored flags that floated from roof, and tree, and leafy arch. Crowds of villagers came flocking in by the various paths: there were then no roads beyond the town, save one for a portion of the way to the royal palace at Hangurankette. Priests in yellow robes were clustering about the Maligawa; chiefs of all degrees in white and crimson robes, were gathering near the palace, and the little island in the lake was made gay with flowers and music.

The hour of reception was at high noon, and as the time approached, the crowd below became denser and noisier, and the harsh drums and shrieking pipes, belched forth a barbarous melody that made a Saxon's ear feel strangely. It was the Christian's Perraharra, and as the captive object of all this turmoil walked slowly and calmly, almost sorrowfully, towards the busy scene, he was followed by a wandering army of gazers, most of whom looked upon a white man for the first time. Miles of white cloths, acres of bright red, oceans of many colored drapery were spread along the dusty ground or festooned along the shabby walls and palace. About the latter all was hushed as a sleeping child: they had a rather unpleasant way of stopping noises in that part of his Majesty's dominions, which generally proved efficacious. The stillness that was scarcely human, was in ill-keeping with the fiendish pictures on the temple walls close by, on which were painted plaintive shrieks and groans and other issuings of human agony.

At noon precisely, it pleased his Kandyan Majesty to come forth. His subjects received him as an Oriental race ever received a despot who delights in the royal game of "heads and tails." They received him with a great deal of feeling, especially about the region of the neck. They held their breath as he drew near, felt a tightness about their throats as he passed, and when he had gone on his way, men involuntarily raised their hands and their heads to make quite certain that they were in their right place. Raja Singha rode the royal coach, a present from the English Governor, the British captive walking by his side. That was a wonderful coach, the Lord Mayor's was as nothing to it; gold and glass, and precious stones, and silver bells, and velvet cushions, and gold lace, were on it, and many other things too precious to be put on paper, but not too precious to be sold by an old Dutch auctioner in Colombo, whither it was despatched piece-meal after the capture of the city by the British. Four stately black horses drew the carriage at funeral pace to the "Hall of Seals" where Rajah Singha alighted. The captive also entered followed at a respectful distance by the royal betel-box and the imperial spittoon, the gold stick and silver spoon in waiting, the royal Ministers, aud scores, of Lord Lieutenants and Deputy Lieutenants of counties. Seated in his chair of State, the King motioned the captive to stand near his royal person, and bade him watch the evolutions of the imperial coach and four, and the wheeling past of the household brigade of Plantain Eaters. There was one small band of thirty-two amidst the motley troops, which marched past, a gloomy band of ruffians, nearly nude and carrying grim-looking instruments in their hands. These were the royal torturers, each of the thirty-two having a different grade of the art of torment to inflict. They carried human gridirons, toasting forks of Cyclopean dimensions, awkward looking surgical and dentists' instruments, and as these thirty-two scowled on the people, the crowd shrank back in hate and terror!

Upon the whole it was a gala sight; there were as many jewels about the royal person and the chair of State, as would have established an ordinary jeweller in business. But nobody cared much about the jewels, or the chair of State; they gazed intently at the royal face, for smiles there meant promotion, frowns something very different. The captive was arrayed by royal command in the uniform of a general officer who had recently been waylaid and knocked over in the low country. The lords of the household wore their best coronation robes, and the headmen were marvels of greatness about the body; to see the miles of snow white cloth about them, you might have taken them for cotton lords, or looking at their enormous rotundity, that each one was a lord-mayor with his "corporation." The captive thought not of the military rabble, and the glass coach and four, but when questioned he replied to royalty like a book read backwards, and as it happened that his Majesty had partaken of a good omelet curry that morning, there was not a life missing when all was over. Every one carried home his head between his shoulders. And so the barbarous band struck up a dismal clang, the savage troops fired their rusty ginghalls, the people shouted, the royal elephants sent forth their shrieking cries, flags waved and weapons glistened in the noon-day sun: but he in whose honor all this turmoil rose, heeded it not. He saw but one small group of tiny figures, playing as last he saw them on a bright autumn day—his own loved children, on the grass beneath the apple-trees!

* * * * *

Twelve months passed away, and another Christmas Day arrived: again the bright blue sky and morning breeze, and flowers, and palm trees welcomed all living things; but they welcomed not the captive. Lenna was there *alone*, still gazing westward for the coming of those whose faith was her own.

Behind the shady tamarind tree, in a quiet nook, there was a grave on which the grass was fresh.

* * * * *

Five years later when British troops planted Old England's flag upon the royal palace, men asked abont the captive aud his home. They were shewn the humble cottage then in ruins, and the quiet spot behind the tamarind tree. A group of officers was seen standing around the spot uncovered; there were then *two* graves!

MY PEARL FISHING EXPEDITION.

ON the 25th February, 18—, I arrived in the Bay of Condatchy, the anchorage of Aripo, a passenger on board the Government barque "Wellington." The Superintendant of the Pearl Banks had invited me to accompany him, and I had gladly accepted the offer.

Early the next morning, I landed with the Superintendant at Silawatorre, a small village distant a few miles from the station at Aripo. This was a most miserable little place consisting of but a single row of small mud huts standing in hot and dusty solitude, with topes of shady palms near them; but far as the eye could reach inland or coastwise, there was nothing to break the monotony of endless palm plains save the distant white walls of the "Doric;" a lofty stuccoed government building at some distance, which glistened and shone brilliantly in the rays of the morning sun.

There were a few dirty women, and thin-faced childreu on the beach, whose curiosity had for the moment overcome their sloth. Further on under some palms, stood the Adapanaar of Aripo or head man of the district; a fine grey-bearded old native, attended by his deputy the Maniagar, and a few seedy-looking followers armed to the teeth with paper umbrellas and painted sticks. The Superintendant adjourned with these strange-looking officials to a thatched open bungalow by a small flag-staff, where they were soon engrossed in details respecting the approaching fishery. The scene was altogether so desolate and uninteresting, and the sun was becoming so powerful, that I was glad to return to the ship by the first opportunity.

The following morning we stood out for the banks near which the anchor was dropped, and for several days the Superintendant and his boat's crew were occupied in placing buoys with little blue and red flags attached, upon the edges of the several beds which were to be fished. The weather was oppressively hot; the sky was without a cloud to break the intensity of the sun's rays.

On the 5th of March we returned to our anchorage in Condatchy Bay; but this time closer to the shore. What a

change had come over the place! The very sands of the plain seemed to be redolent of life. The miserable row of low, dirty huts had either been levelled to the ground or were hidden from sight by numberless gaily-coloured booths of all sorts of shapes, and sizes, ornamented with pale green leaves of the palmyrah and cocoa palm and long strips of white cloth. There were thousands of natives flocking and struggling down to the beach, as though they expected us to bring on shore all the wealth of the pearl banks. Our anchorage-ground was opposite the little flag-staff; and about us as thick as they could be moored, lay fully two hundred native boats of various sizes, though of one build, being a short rakish-looking barge; so sharp and knowing, both forwards and aft, that one might have imagined them to have been bloated London wherries. They were each manned by ten oarsmen, a tindal or steersman and his deputy, besides a cooly for baling out the water, for most of these craft leak freely. They measure from eight to twelve tons, yet there are very few nails about them, the omnipotent cocoanut fibre serving to fasten nearly all Indian vessels and boats together.

After a lapse of four days spent by the Superintendant, the magistrate of the district, the government agent, and the Adapanaar in various arrangements; in publishing notices and issuing instructions connected with the fishery—the first diving day was fixed, and the boats to the number of two hundred, were forthwith in readiness.

The day previous to the fishery, the "Wellington" once more stood out for the banks with the Superintendant and his boat's crew on board. The boats with their respective complements of divers, were to leave precisely at midnight, so as to arrive on the banks before day-light, the wind being at that time off the land and in their favour. In order to see as much as possible of their proceedings, I remained to accompany the fleet with the old Adapanaar in his ten-oared cutter. I lay down at dusk in a small shed attached to the temporary military quarters, intending to snatch a few hours' repose. But I soon found sleep was quite out of the question; I walked out and found the boatmen and divers far from attempting any rest previous to their heavy labours, merry-making on the sea-beach. Some were dancing, some beating time on the tom-tom; scores were chaunting their wild songs, and all had been well supplied with toddy and arrack. The night was pitchy dark, and but few stars were visible over the bright glare of many torches. A huge bonfire blazed over the flag-staff, lighting up bazaars, palm-trees, and temples in one lurid glare, and flinging a few rays on the distant shining walls on the Doric. The shark-charmer too, stood in all his glory, on the summit of one of the vast heaps of blanched oyster shells: he was holding forth to the assembled crowd with shouts and wild gesticulations, and as the glare of the fire shot past him, he appeared to be clothed in flame, whilst his gaunt arms flung long shadows over the distant plain, like those of a monster windmill hard at work in the midnight breeze.

The appointed time drew near; a gong sent forth a few notes of thunder; and instantly all noises ceased. The shark-charmer stole away, no one knew where; some thought to pray, more probably into the arrack bazaar; the boatmen, divers, and government peons crowding down the beach and through the water, passed to their appointed posts in the boats. More than four thousand human beings packed themselves into those frail-looking craft; and yet they were not so crowded as not to leave room for the oysters.

The Adapanaar gave the final signal amidst a momentary hush; a small field-piece was fired from the base of the flag-staff; and away went one hundred boats in gallant style! A loud discordant shout was raised on shore, answered lustily by the crews and divers, and all was still again. The land breeze was fresh: the water was smooth as glass; and our fleet made rapid way. The large yellow bamboo masts pointed high in air, with their enormous, beautifully white, transparent sails filling with the breeze, and lit up by the bonfire on shore, seemed as though they were a host of huge winged creatures of the deep.

On the soft cushions of our roomy craft I laid me down beneath the awning's shade and slept some quiet hours. I started from my rest on hearing some one near me giving orders in a loud voice. It was still dark and looking out I perceived a bright small light not very far distant. It was a signal-light at the mast-head of the "Wellington." We were close to the "banks" and in a few minutes I was on board the vessel. The fleet went astern, and there quietly awaited day-light. By the time we had sipped a cup of hot coffee, and smoked a cheroot, it was day-dawn, and then a move was made. I passed once more to the soft cushions of the cutter, the Adapanaar saw all ready, and in a few minutes a gun was fired and off we went as before.

The fishing-grounds lay above half a mile a-head of the bark, and arriving on them it occupied some time to arrange the many boats in proper order, so as to prevent delay or confusion. The sun was rising bright and gorgeous over the land. All eyes were turned towards the "Wellington," awaiting the expected signal to commence operations, five divers in each boat were mounted on the gunwales armed with their diving stones, nets and ropes; the remaining five stood eagerly watching them. The Superintendent was standing on the vessel's poop, the boatswain by his side with the signal halyards in his hands. Minutes seemed hours. At last there was a move on the deck, and the signal-flag rose slowly upwards; the Union-jack fluttered in the morning breeze, and just as it touched the mast-head, five hundred divers, with their stones and nets, plunged silently in the sea. I shall not easily forget the sensation I experienced when I saw the crowd of human beings disappear in the depths below, leaving but a few bubbles to mark their downward path. I pulled out my watch; a quarter of a minute elapsed, and not one of all the hundreds appeared; then a half, and then three quarters; still not one rose to the surface. I turned to the Adapanaar in a tremor of anxiety, but he was sitting calm and quiet as an oyster. How gladly my heart beat when I saw first a dozen heads and shoulders, then fifty, then a hundred and more, ascend to the surface, bubbling and spluttering, as well they might, after such a submarine excursion. And the bustle and excitement began in good earnest, on all sides. The boatmen helped to pull in the baskets full of oysters; the divers, but little fatigued, climbed over the boats' sides and saw their fish counted into distinct heaps by the peon in charge of the boat. Each appeared to have brought up from fifty to seventy oysters. As the last of the divers came over the boats' sides, the five hundred who had quietly waited their turn rose up and, with their baskets and stones, plunged in as their comrades had before them, as rapidly and as silently.

The arrangements for diving are exceedingly simple:—the diving-stone is a piece of granite, conical-shaped, and weighing about ten pounds; through one end of it a double cord of coir is rove, of sufficient length to reach the bottom easily, one end of it being secured to the boat. When about plunging in, the diver places his right foot on the stone and between the double cord, using it as a stirrup; the weight suffices to hasten his descent, and on arriving at the bottom the stone is cast away and pulled up by the boatmen, so as to be clear of the basket rope: this rope is stouter, and single. The diver seizes the hoop of the basket firmly between the toes of his left foot—for the natives use their toes as actively as we do our fingers—and when on the bank below, grasps the basket in his left hand flings himself flat on his face, and sweeps the oysters rapidly into his coir bag with his right hand. When he has secured sufficient fish, he gives his comrades above the signal by jerking the rope; they immediately commence hauling it in. To give himself an impetus upwards, the diver lays hold of the rope for a second or two, then raises his hand together above his head, and rapidly floats to the surface.

The day's work over, the fleet pushed shorewards, the breeze came up from the south-west fitfully at first, then steadily: up went the great spider-legged bamboo masts, and the wide-winged sails, and the sharp-nosed boats slipped noiselessly landwards.

The whole of the fleet having reached the shore, a party of Malay riflemen and peons, cleared an open space between them and the crowd on the beach, so as to allow the unloading of the boats, which was at once commenced. The oysters were divided on the sandy shore, into four equal parts, three of which went to the Government, the remaining fourth was shared amongst the boatmen, the divers, the tindal and the boat-owner; the divers receiving twice as much as the boat-men, and the owners rather more than the divers. The Government oysters were carried up in basket to large bamboo enclosures called cottoos, where they were kept until sold by auction on the following day. The other share of the fish was disposed of in a similar way; though, sometimes, they were retained by their owners on their own account, and the pearls found in them sold afterwards.

There were many wealthy traders there from all parts of India; but many more had with difficulty scraped together sums varying from a dozen pagodas to a dozen dollars; men who had purchased or borrowed the means of bidding at this intoxicating auction: men who had left their famished families without the means of obtaining a mouthful of rice: who had torn the gold bangles and ear-rings from their wives and children, and melted them into ingots to deal in the maddening trade of Aripo. Some returned home rich beyond their expectations: but many went back ruined, beggared, and broken-hearted, unable to repay their loans, while some fled in terror to strange lands, having lost the means of replacing monies taken by them from sources of trust—ruined in means and reputation. All this happens at every pearl fishery, and is not to be prevented, save by offering the fish in larger lots; which, though it might not prove quite so remunerative to the Government, would save much evil and suffering.

Some conception may be formed of the immense masses of oysters which at these times lay putrifying on the burning sands of Aripo, when I mention that each boat will bring on shore, in one trip, from ten to twenty thousands of fish, making a daily total of from one to two millions for the whole fleet. The extremely hazardous results of these auctions may be gathered from the fact, that whilst in some instances as many as six pearls of various weights and values are found in one oyster of large size, one hundred oysters may be opened without finding in them a single pearl.

The natives of India have a singular belief with regard to the origin of pearls: it is, that those beautiful concretions are congealed dew-drops, which Buddha, in certain months, showers upon the earth, and are caught by the oysters whilst floating on the waters to breathe. The priests, ever alive to their own interests, keep up the strange belief, and make it the pretext for exacting from the divers and boatmen of their faith what are termed "charity oysters" for the use of Buddah, who, when thus propitiated, according to their showing, will render the fish more rich in pearls in future seasons.